SAMUEL BARBER
65 Songs

Edited by Richard Walters

ED 4453

ISBN 978-1-4234-9126-2

G. SCHIRMER, Inc.

DISTRIBUTED BY

HAL•LEONARD®
CORPORATION
7777 W. BLUEMOUND RD. P.O. BOX 13819 MILWAUKEE, WI 53213

www.schirmer.com
www.halleonard.com

CONTENTS

SONGS PUBLISHED DURING THE COMPOSER'S LIFETIME

In chronological order of publication

SONGS PUBLISHED POSTHUMOUSLY

[1] First published in this edition
[2] First published in *Samuel Barber: Ten Early Songs* (1994)
[3] First published in *Samuel Barber: Ten Selected Songs* (2008)

APPENDIX 1: MANUSCRIPT FACSIMILES OF SELECTED EARLY SONGS

APPENDIX 2: THE DAISIES

Samuel Barber in his studio at the American Academy in Rome, 1953.

NOTICE to *Mother and nobody else*

Dear Mother: I have written this to tell you my worrying secret. Now don't cry when you read it because it is neither yours nor my fault. I suppose I will have to tell it now without any nonsense. To begin with I was not meant to be an athlet [sic]. I was meant to be a composer, and will be I'm sure. I'll ask you one more thing.— Don't ask me to try to forget this unpleasant thing and go play football.— *Please* — Sometimes I've been worrying about this so much that it makes me mad (not very),

> Love,
> Sam Barber II
> [written at age 9]

CONTENTS
Alphabetically

POET INDEX

ABOUT THE EDITION

Samuel Barber left a substantial number of early compositions unpublished during his lifetime. For whatever reasons, he had preferences about which works he publicly acknowledged, signaled by their publication. This is a common pattern among composers, particularly in the 20th century. The unpublished compositions clearly meant something to him, however. While a few manuscripts of songs are indeed lost, he kept copies of most unpublished works throughout his life. As an adult he even occasionally fondly recopied a piece composed in childhood or his teenage years.

At this writing we are now past the one-hundredth anniversary of Barber's birth, and nearly 30 years after his death. His career and work have clearly become historical, and interest in his complete output is inevitable. One would not expect Barber's previously unpublished songs to have the sophistication of his mature work. Yet in them we see the composer's talent for melody, for setting text, and for capturing sincerely felt emotion. These are qualities found in all his songs, early and late. Barber had a sure sense of writing for the voice from the beginning. This is not something that can be taught, after all. The compositions of the teenaged Barber reveal a remarkably sensitive and cultured creator. One can sense music he was absorbing, particularly the work of his uncle Sidney Homer, the sentimental music of the era, Brahms lieder, and many other influences. Even as a boy Barber had the natural ability to produce a completely conceived and realized work of art, unhampered by self-consciousness; this is almost never the case with a young composer. Barber's youthful work lacks any hint of someone trying to prove himself, also unusual for someone of that age. If for no other reason, the previously unpublished early works are valuable clues as to how a great composer developed.

The previously released *Samuel Barber: Collected Songs* included all the songs published during Barber's lifetime, totaling 36. All appear in this edition. The additional *Samuel Barber: Ten Early Songs* was released in 1994, included here. In 2008 in *Samuel Barber: Ten Selected Songs*, two further early songs were published, which appear here. The present edition adds 17 more songs to the published works of Barber.

In choosing unpublished songs for inclusion in this edition it was necessary to be selective up to a point. Almost all songs composed from the age of 15 on, for which a manuscript source could be located, have been included in this edition. An exception is "Song for a New House" (1940) for voice, flute and piano. Permission for inclusion could not be obtained; we hope to release an edition of it in the future. A few songs composed at the age of 14 (*Two Poems of the Wind*, for example) have been included. As samplings of earlier work, facsimiles are included in an appendix.

MUSICAL SOURCES

Manuscripts of all songs in this collection were consulted, as well as the few marked proofs that survive. Sources were the Library of Congress, the Eastman School of Music, the Chester County Historical Society, and the Curtis Institute of Music.

RESEARCH SOURCES

This edition owes a great debt to the research of Barbara Heyman, the leading Barber scholar. Her work includes a biography, *Samuel Barber: The Composer and His Music* (Oxford University Press, 1992), and *A Comprehensive Thematic Catalog of the Works of Samuel Barber* (consulted in manuscript, publication forthcoming as of this writing in 2010). These two books were a principal source for the notes on the songs. I urge anyone interested in the topic to read Barbara Heyman's books for more in depth detail about Barber's music and career.

Many other additional sources were consulted, among them: *Samuel Barber: A Guide to Research* by Wayne C. Wentzel (Routledge, 2001); *Samuel Barber Remembered: A Centenary Tribute* edited by Peter Dickinson (University of Rochester Press, 2010); "Samuel Barber: An Improvisatory Portrait," essay by Paul Wittke, published at www.schirmer.com.

A GENERAL EDITORIAL NOTE

For all works published in his lifetime, Barber commonly made changes on the publisher's proofs, creating differences from manuscript sources. Note content changes were very rare. These proofreading changes generally regard musical indications, tempos and dynamics. This last step before publication was an obvious and logical chance for the composer to deliberately clarify his intentions. This process is common among published composers.

Most of the marked proofs are lost. Noting the differences between the manuscript sources and the published versions, one can guess at the changes that Barber must have made on the proofs. Changes to proofs continued throughout Barber's career, but are particularly heavy in the earliest published works. We do not attempt to annotate these details in the "Notes on the Songs" section of this edition. However, as an example, the following paragraph cites the differences in the manuscript and the published edition of "Bessie Bobtail."

A metronome marking does not appear on Barber's manuscript. Barber's ms. shows the meter as cut time, changed by the Schirmer editor to 2/2. These do not appear in the manuscript, but were added on proofs: *poco f* in m. 18, swell and *f* mm. 23-25; cresc. *poco a poco* in mm. 33-34 over the vocal line; swells in voice and piano parts mm.36-37; *f* in m. 38; *f* over vocal line in m. 41; swell in m. 43; *ff* in piano part, m. 43; poco allarg. in m. 43; Barber's manuscript shows *f* for the voice at the end of m. 43, changed to *ff* on proofs; the articulations in the piano part in measures 40-43 were presumably added on proofs. The manuscript shows *f* in piano part m. 44, presumably changed to *ff* on proofs; *ff* appears in the voice and piano parts in the manuscript in m. 48, deleted on proofs. A *f* appears in the piano part in m. 39, moved on proofs to m. 38.

Throughout the edition any breath marks, piano fingerings, or piano pedaling indications are Barber's. Editorial input, suggestion or clarification is shown throughout in brackets.

I would like to thank and acknowledge the following for their valuable assistance in making this edition: the Library of Congress, Eastman School of Music, the Curtis Institute of Music, Laura Ward, Joel Boyd, David Flachs, and especially assistant editor Joshua Parman.

Richard Walters
Editor

FOREWORD

Editor's Note: *Paul Wittke was Samuel Barber's editor at G. Schirmer for decades, and also the composer's friend. In 1994, near the end of his long career at Schirmer, Paul Wittke wrote an extraordinary, free-wheeling essay about Barber, in which he not only discusses his music, but creates a vivid personal portrait. After months of research on the topic and several drafts of a foreword for this volume, it became apparent to me that nothing I wrote could possibly be as compelling as Wittke's essay, drenched in personal knowledge and experience with the composer. It has been excerpted and slightly adapted in the form which appears below. In general, sections about orchestral, instrumental works and operas have been omitted. The essay may be read in its entirety at www.schirmer.com.*

Richard Walters
Editor

SAMUEL BARBER:
AN IMPROVISATORY PORTRAIT

Essay by Paul Wittke

© 1994 by G. Schirmer, Inc.
excerpted and adapted with permission

In any pantheon of American musicians, Samuel Barber (1910–1981) commands a prominent niche. Along with the works of Aaron Copland and George Gershwin, his are the most often played. He has become almost popular — a word that would make him cringe. Barber would be amused and amazed by all this, for he often called himself "a living dead" American composer.

During the heady years of our musical adolescence, the 1930s and '40s, he was virtually ignored in any book of American musical life, relegated to a polite and often ungracious footnote, for not believing in raising the decibel of aural shockwaves. He remained a maverick romantic lyricist in a turbulent age. Furthermore, he committed the unpardonable sin of being a cosmopolitan when most composers were belligerently American, or took refuge in European techniques that have no relationship to the American psyche. In our current pluralistic climate, when it is no longer fashionable to denigrate any compositional style, Barber is home free.

The famous brouhaha of the 1930s is now moldy history. Ashley Pettis in *The New York Times* lambasted Arturo Toscanini for performing Barber's music — the *Adagio for Strings*, no less — and accused Barber of being an antediluvian anachronism. The squabble subsided when Roy Harris — who in no way shared Barber's aesthetics — came to his defense, and said "conservatism and advanced music could and should live as a harmonious happy couple." Barber in return called Harris the father of the American Symphony.

It took courage to be Samuel Barber in the 1940s; he said so himself. This was the time of the emerging giants — Copland, Thomson, Sessions, Piston, Carter, and company. But despite the derision of his enemies no one ever denied his polished style, or his integrity, nor did they resent his honesty in admitting he wanted to reach a large musical audience. In this he was more than successful.

A lot of nonsense has been written about Barber's music, some overly adulatory and some unseemingly nasty. When all the rhetoric is washed away, what is significant is that his music is now valued as a priceless contribution to our musical history. And what is most important and becoming increasingly apparent is the fact that he was a far more complex man and musician than he has been given credit for; beneath his charm he was deadly serious about his art and had no interest "in superficial nonsense," by which he meant most of the intellectual and musical currents floating around at that time. He belonged to no school, clique, or organization, and (except for his association with Gian Carlo Menotti) went his own solitary way, never a denizen of the boardroom or the locker room. Undoubtedly he had the same inner conflicts that confront any dedicated artist, although his talent was recognized early. Particularly after the Toscanini affiliation many critics did not understand that Barber marched to a different drummer. He was never a camp follower of anyone. One of the few musicians who always recognized his individuality was William Schuman, who remained a staunch admirer of Barber's music throughout their lives.

To our sound bite generation, Barber's life is devoid of any excitement. He was never a minor subsidiary figure in even a mildly lurid scandal, he shunned the glamour of partisan musical and non-musical politics, he gave no lectures, he wrote no books, he was not a performer — although he began his career as a singer — and he did not teach, except for two years at Curtis which he said he heartily disliked. He went his own merry (some would say morose) way. He did nothing but compose, a rare privilege in a profession that does not allow for any overabundance of luxuries.

Certainly in the early years he was in many ways the spoiled darling of the gods. He was born into a comfortable, educated, social, and distinguished American family (he was related to Robert Fulton) in West Chester, Pennsylvania on 9 March 1910. He was spared the virtues of poverty and never enjoyed the values of starving in a garret. His father was a doctor, an Episcopalian pillar of society, his mother was a sensitive amateur pianist; his aunt, Louise Homer, a leading contralto at the Metropolitan Opera, was married to Sidney Homer, a respectable composer of American art songs. Perhaps more than anybody it was Homer who molded the integrity and aesthetic values of his nephew. When he died in 1953 Barber was profoundly grieved.

Barber, an uncommonly bright boy, was unduly pampered and spoiled. He retained the art of playing stage center; he never fully outgrew these years, and remained a master of attracting friends who, as he did, indulged in caviar and champagne. In his teens at Curtis he was a triple threat prodigy of composition, voice, and piano and became a favorite of Mary Louise Curtis Bok, founder of the school. It was she who introduced him to the Schirmer family (his only publisher) and later helped him to acquire Capricorn, his home in Mount Kisco, New York. At Curtis he met Gian Carlo Menotti, a 17-year-old Italian youth, recommended to the school by Toscanini. In 1928 his winning a prize from Columbia University for his Violin Sonata financed a trip to Europe. His interest in European life and culture now blossomed into a full blown love affair. Forever after he felt equally at home on two continents.

After the success of his early *Overture to the School for Scandal* (1931), *Music for a Scene from Shelley* (1933), *Adagio for Strings* (1936), *First Symphony in One Movement* (1936), *First Essay* (1937) and *Violin Concerto* (1939) he did not have to beg for performances by the world's leading conductors — Arturo Toscanini, Eugene Ormandy, Dimitri Mitropoulos, Bruno Walter, Charles Munch, George Szell, Artur Rodzinski, Leopold Stokowski, and Thomas Schippers. And most of his compositions were commissioned or first performed by such artists as Vladimir Horowitz, Eleanor Steber, Raya Garbousova, John Browning, Leontyne Price, Pierre Bernac, Francis Poulenc, and Dietrich Fischer-Dieskau. His life until the unwarranted disaster of *Antony and Cleopatra* (1966) was a series of triumphs.

Favored though he was, to those who could pierce the shell of his courtly reserve and tolerate the barbs of his waspish tongue, he was a loyal friend, a fantastic conversationalist, and an endlessly entertaining companion. On the one hand he was resourceful in annoying his enemies and on the other, found many subtle ways to display the bonds of friendship. Difficult as he sometimes was, his friends were legion. Barber was in many ways a double man who seemed to live in two simultaneous time warps. Often, he was with you and yet he was not; even so he always managed to be polite and solicitous. Far from being mollycoddled and flighty he could be tough; he was adept at getting what he wanted, not in a burly, aggressive marketplace manner, but swathed in charm, humor, deftness, masterminded by a keen pragmatic intelligence.

He was truly cultivated, with an encyclopedic knowledge of art, literature, music, and more than a few other subjects. Fluent in languages, he read Proust in French, Goethe in German, Dante in Italian, Neruda in Spanish and *Moby Dick* in Italian (at least he said he did). Barber agreed with Flaubert that literature was a perpetual orgy. At one time he seriously thought of becoming a writer, and the few extant letters we have are written with the panache of a born writer — spontaneous, perceptive, funny, concrete. (In this ability he is in the class of Benjamin Britten and Virgil Thomson.) He often casually mentioned that the son of one of his benefactors, Mrs. Bok, in a fit of jealousy, destroyed all his youthful letters to her. Although he understood in hindsight the jealousy behind this act, he very much regretted that it happened for much of the history of his early years was irrevocably lost. Fortunately at the same time he was writing often and copiously to his Uncle Sidney. These letters have been preserved by one of Homer's daughters and so we do have a glimpse, if tepid and guarded, of his formative years. Homer was a beloved relative, and of a more conservative generation. Barber could be more candid with the more modern Mrs. Bok.

Barber was a fervent devotee of gossip, even in his reading. Autobiographies, journals, the diaries of everyone from Rousseau, Pepys, Thoreau, Tolstoy, Dostoyevsky (he was partial to anything Russian) to Churchill, letters of the Marquise de Sévigné, Darwin, or Hart Crane. An avid subscriber to magazines, he absorbed everything from *Vanity Fair* and *The Smithsonian* to the scholarly literary journals, especially *Botteghe Oscure*. This handsome, multi-language periodical, printed in Rome, was famous for publishing every important and about-to-be important writer of its day (the 1930s and 40s) in their original languages. He read the text of James Agee's *Knoxville: Summer of 1915* when it was first published in the pages of the new-born *Partisan Review*, a journal destined to become the fountainhead of the New York intelligentsia. Barber was an avid admirer of Trollope and read all of the Barchester series (long before they were discovered by "Masterpiece Theatre"). The "New York Edition" of Henry James was one of his prized possessions. But he was no antiquarian and kept abreast of contemporary literature.

He was no bookworm, no remote stuffy intellectual; he had nothing in common with horn-rimmed scholars entombed in unairconditioned libraries. He wore his learning with a light and phosphorescent wit. But his moods were unpredictable. You never knew when he would shift from a serious discussion of Bach cantatas to a zany impulse, suggesting to "go to Sweden and find out if Strindberg really was an alchemist" or "take a tramp steamer to see it rain in the Rain Forest."

One thing was positively off limits; you could not discuss his music with him, particularly works in progress. If you penetrated this sacred domain, you were lucky to escape unscathed with a "Well, I'm writing some Czerny etudes" (the Piano Sonata) or "something incestuous, you'll love it" (*Andromache's Farewell*) or "a setting from your Bible" (*Fadograph*, from *Finnegans Wake*). Music was his life, his private world, and he carefully guarded any attempt to breach the ramparts. If you even hinted at the subject, he would regale you with a complete, soulful recounting of his "servant problem." The machination of his chauffeur and his eternally pregnant wife (Barber's cook) fascinated him. He unquestionably loved them, was fascinated by their quotidian problems, and solved their difficulties in many, sometimes costly, ways.

He was an astute art, theater, and film critic, was well-versed in painting and did a bit of it himself. He drew very well and if he thought you were interested in these "dabblings" and not the man who produced them, he would show you his temperas. Barber was unusually modest, and his art works had a touching, poetic quality that he only revealed to his very close acquaintances.

Barber's relationship with other composers such as Virgil Thomson and Aaron Copland was generally polite but occasionally the crossing could be rough. Composers in the Roger Sessions camp brushed him aside and he returned their compliments bite by bite. Even with people he greatly admired, like Leonard Bernstein, there were awkward moments. He was always courteous but his scabrous wit, often coiled in honeyed sentences, was not always appreciated. Yet there was no question that most of his colleagues respected him, as he reciprocated in kind.

In spite of his famous quip, "How awful that the artist has become nothing but the after-dinner mint of society," he was not notoriously plebeian. He loved to hobnob with the wealthy and famous provided they had intellects to match. This well-bred American felt very much at ease with Princess Bassiano who financed *Botteghe Oscure*, Countess de Polignac, the reigning patroness of Paris, and whose salon was de rigueur for the intelligentsia of the 1920s and '30s, and Vicomtesse de Marie-Laure Noailles, a friend of many modern artists and musicians.

Never one to man the barricades, he did enter the political arena on two memorable occasions. He was president of the International Music Council of UNESCO, where he did much to bring into focus and ameliorate the conditions of international musical problems. He was one of the first American composers to visit Russia, where he became a friend of Shostakovich, who later visited him at Capricorn. Barber was also influential in the successful campaign of serious composers against ASCAP. Through his and other musicians' efforts, serious composers increased the share of royalties they receive from their compositions.

When Barber entered a room you knew he was a presence. His penetrating brown eyes took in every nook, cranny, and paper clip, and for a fraction of a second you felt like a suspect in a police lineup. Then the eyes became warm, his hands outstretched, and he gave you an almost annihilating bear hug. After the usual amenities, he would confide some impish bit of misconduct. Rapidly the conversation became more cordial, and soon you were enmeshed in serious discussion, interloaded with much laughter and salacious banter. Barber was always a challenge to be with. In some ways, he was a victim of over-refinement, and in later years could pass for a rather decadent Russian nobleman. But he was essentially very American; he had the curmudgeonly mien of the mature Henry James or Edmund Wilson. There is no doubt that he came from the same mold.

The first overtly titled piece is *Dover Beach* (1931). It is important in Barber's biography. He was then a trained singer and had a beautiful baritone voice. Vaughan Williams heard him perform it at Bryn Mawr College, admired the work, and encouraged Barber to continue to compose. *Dover Beach* is also another proof that Barber's melancholy was endemic to his nature. Why else should a young man of 21 choose to set such a bleak poem as Matthew Arnold's? He was a solitary child, preferring to read and live in his own world rather than engage in athletics. The sports he did indulge in were noncombative — hiking, skiing, ice skating, swimming. He had no taste for the American desire to win every game in which he participated. Quite the contrary, competition in this sense was anathema to his inborn solitary nature. *Dover Beach* represents Barber's first work in an extended form for voice and ensemble — a form that he was to become a master of; in this case the ensemble was a string quartet rather than orchestra. *Knoxville: Summer of 1915* (1947), *Andromache's Farewell* (1962), and *Two Scenes from Antony and Cleopatra* (1966) are Barber at his best.

Barber always retained the benefits of his vocal training. His speaking voice was beautifully modulated, if at times too self-consciously mid-Atlantic. His singing must have been more than adequate in 1956 to impress Rudolf Bing, when he sang him the score of *Vanessa* (1957). Although the opera had not been previously commissioned, the impresario was so astonished he accepted and produced the work. Barber also had an improvising skill at creating his own folk music, seemingly authentic songs that he would sing in a poker-faced, benign manner with unprintable lyrics to match.

In *Knoxville: Summer of 1915* (1947) he put his heart on the line. James Agee's text and Barber's music are so sturdily wedded that it is difficult to separate them. It is a rueful and nostalgic recreation of our lost innocence. The sane and sanitized world of Barber's West Chester and Agee's southern town is made palpable to us all.

Actually, West Chester was no cultural backwater. It was near Philadelphia and Barber had easy access to its offerings, and always retained a soft spot for the city; it played a major part in his education, and was a definitive part of his background. Barber had the advantages of both sides of the American genteel years. Like the James brothers and Wallace Stevens (whom he also resembles in some ways) he was a member of a society that observed good manners and believed in the necessity of controlled respectability. It was a milieu that took life and its obligations seriously, but added a generous helping of intelligent conversation and hearty laughter.

Barber never gave any spoken indication of a religious belief. But his orthodox Presbyterian-Quaker background left a deep-rooted imprint on him. We can sense this in his choice of such texts as *Hermit Songs* (1953) and *Prayers of Kierkegaard*. True, the *Hermit Songs* poems, written by medieval monks, are both sacred and profane, but the majority of them lean toward an attitude of simple faith. They may also be interpreted as examples of the isolated lonely life of an artist as well as a religious. The last text ("Alone I came into the world") is touched with the ironic humor characteristic of Barber. In *Hermit Songs*, like *Die Natali*, faith is taken for granted, situated within rigid Christian bounds.

But *Prayers of Kierkegaard* is unequivocally a religious statement. Here the no-nonsense realistic-yet-hopeful attitude of American Protestantism, the nucleus of Barber's upbringing, has found a center. He wrote, in discussing the work: "One finds here three basic truths(:) imagination, dialectic, and religious melancholy. The truth he [Kierkegaard] sought after was a truth which was a truth for me." Can any definition of a faith be clearer?

In both of these works Barber conveys the passing of time in subtle ways, and not only by his individual use of Gregorian chant. ("For me, it is the most religious music possible.") Is it a misreading of *Hermit Songs* to note that the medieval experience of time, experienced in the here and now (immanence), is expressed by the absolute absence of metric notation in the entire cycle? The notated *Prayers of Kierkegaard* also has Gregorian elements but ends with a four-square chorale. In the Protestant world, time is linear and is experienced as a process of life's unpredictability but with a promise of a divine heaven (transcendence). It seems that Barber, by his own admission, reveals he is at heart a good Presbyterian.

Love and its pitfalls are the subtext of many of his vocal compositions from the James Joyce *Chamber Music* song cycle (1936) to the bitter, subjective *Despite and Still* cycle (1969). It is subtly suggested in the *Mélodies Passagères* (1950-51), written when he boasted "he was in love" (again).

Barber had a native passion for Celtic, particularly Irish, literature. His first songs were settings of James Stephens; one of his last works was based on a quotation from James Joyce. *Reincarnations*, acknowledged as a masterpiece of American choral literature, also has a text by James Stephens. The *Hermit Songs* are medieval Celtic. Barber considered himself a throwback Irishman. He loved the land and its people, their melancholy strain, their wild humor, their verbal felicity.

Barber was a great admirer of Yeats, especially the world-weary, realistic poet of the late years, not the spirit-guided author of "The Vision." (Oddly enough he set only one of his poems, "The Secrets of the Old.") He apparently had a minor epiphany at the poet's grave at Bulbec. The beauty of the surroundings, the out-of-time atmosphere, made the imaginative power of Yeats's poetry come patently alive for him there. He told the story often and very movingly. Yeats and Barber are in no way comparable, but on some atavistic level they share the Irish soul.

James Joyce, the antithesis of Yeats, was of equal importance to Barber. He was a close reader of Joyce and familiar with many of the books about him and his work. As early as 1936 he composed his first mini-drama of love long lost, the setting of three poems from *Chamber Music*, Op. 10.

"Nuvoletta" (1947), a witty setting of less obscure words from *Finnegans Wake*, contains a waltz theme that anticipates *Souvenirs*. Barber may not have been as psychologically involved with Joyce as he was with Yeats. This attachment was more intellectual; Joyce's writing is far more complex, and his personality and temperament were somewhat remote from Barber's orientation. But he understood and responded to the poetic mixture of gaiety and sadness that permeates the Joycean canon and that is abundant in his own music.

Many American composers besides Barber have made important contributions to our art song literature — Griffes, Rorem, Hoiby, Thomson, Ives, Copland, Bernstein, et al. But Barber's more than any of the others have become staples in the repertoire of concert singers. His love and understanding of the voice never diminished; it is the foundation of his lyricism. He was cradled in song from the beginning, and absorbed all the complexities of its essence from Sidney and Louise Homer. His own, never-realized singing career, and his symbiotic friendship with Menotti, another natural practitioner of vocal writing, augmented his instinctual gift. His discriminating literary taste, his proficiency with language, and his unending melodic resourcefulness contribute to making his songs so personal, so Barberesque.

If we study all the music Barber has written, an interesting fact becomes discernible. All the compositions he wrote before he was 30 — from the early songs to the pivotal work of his career, the Violin Concerto — give us a synoptic preview of his entire oeuvre. What makes Barber unique is that he discovered himself so early and that all that he added later — allowing for incremental technique devices and the maturing of compositional skills — is already in place.

Capricorn, snug in the hills of Mount Kisco, Westchester County, New York, was Barber's only true home other than the one he was born in at West Chester, Pennsylvania. The coincidental topological conflation of the two locales was not lost on him. He said it "explains a lot about me," for Barber, in spite of his worldliness was "just a small town kid," who only felt comfortable in rural surroundings. He didn't like New York, finding it "the hardest place in the world to write...you become an ornament in the life of New York."

The house itself was simple, elegantly furnished, filled with books, art works, pianos — one that belonged to Rachmaninoff was Barber's prize possession — and manuscripts. Capricorn was actually two independent studios, one for each composer [Barber and Menotti], connected by a central room for living and entertaining. The surrounding grounds were secluded and beautifully landscaped; one could walk and meditate without any disturbance. That it was the home of two famous musicians was recognized by all the neighbors, except for a few uptight do-gooders who thought it was a den of iniquity. (This was 50 years ago, an eon before our age of more relaxed sexual attitudes.) Unquestionably with such a flux of creative talents and temperaments it was not the equivalent of Main Street America. Never boisterous or vulgar, Capricorn was the mecca of the art and intellectual world of Europe and America; to it came a legion of the great, the famous, the talented, and the rich; here they resolved or dissolved their amours and animosities. The two hosts were cordially hospitable to anyone who had something to offer that was new, different, and original.

The volatile, outgoing Menotti always wanted people around him; the reserved West Chesterian, often withdrawn, preferred less excitement. He could tolerate just so much theatricality before delivering one of his coruscating witticisms. But Barber was far from unfriendly or perpetually dour. He could be charming and most amusing, even if his stamina for fun and games was not as extensive as his mercurial friend's.

Capricorn represents the fullest years of the friendship of Barber and Menotti. It was the place where both composers conceived and wrote some of their finest works — Barber's *Medea, Andromache's Farewell*, Piano Sonata, Menotti's *Amahl, The Consul, The Saint of Bleecker Street*.

For a long time it was apparent to close acquaintances of Menotti and Barber that the rupture of their relationship was finally unavoidable. They inhabited different planes of experience and responded to them in completely different emotional ways. These subtle disparities led to their eventual separation. Signs of its dissolution were evident for years and a lot of speculation and rude remarks were made about it. However their friendship was so intimate and complex no one has the right to probe into it. We can only speculate about what could have happened from their public statements, particularly Menotti's. We are aware we are treading in murky and dangerous waters. Although it cannot be denied nor should it be that Menotti was always the central figure in Barber's life, the cause of their separation was not due to any loss of affection for each other. It was simply that as Menotti became more enmeshed in an international operatic world, Barber could not be the only center of Menotti's life.

They were alike and unlike in many ways; both were primarily musical-literary men who fundamentally responded to art (in all its mediums) in basically emotional ways. Barber was more subtle, and saw things always from a broad historical view. Menotti was more immediate and visceral, with both eyes always cocked to the stage. Each had a distinctive gift and style, although occasionally the styles overlapped. Barber, the more innovative of the two, had a sense of proportion and balance only a few composers ever achieve. Paradoxically he appeared on the surface more controlled but was more given to violent outbursts, although some of it was possibly calculated (Barber also had a Barrymore flair). More flamboyant and theatrical, Menotti often had to subdue some of the stormy emotions of the touchy and over-sensitive Barber. This turbulent aspect of their personalities is evident, of course, in the creative works of both composers. Too, the non-operatic Menotti is heir to the wit and clarity of Italian neo-classicism and the erotic mysticism of some aspects of Roman Catholicism. Barber had none of this; his elegance was of a different order, it stemmed from a mind almost French in its clarity and refinement. It is no wonder that Barber could claim "Poulenc was one of my few musical friends. I loved him deeply." Menotti was Italian and Spanish baroque; Barber was elegiac, controlled, compressed. Menotti had the advantage of being able to express himself via the artifacts of the stage; Barber had to rely on mainly musical means to reveal his complicated feelings.

Their friendship began at Curtis when they were in their teens. Menotti, the lonely boy from Italy, soon became a full-fledged member of the Barber family. "Johnny" and Sam were inseparable. Any American trait that Menotti ever acquired was implanted in West Chester. In return, Menotti continentalized Barber, who was internationally inclined and always felt as comfortable in Europe as in America. Menotti has always remained an Italian American and Barber always remained a Europeanized American. In the 1930s they travelled extensively throughout Europe; because they were both multi-lingual and immensely intellectually curious, they felt at home in any country. The zest of their *Wanderjahre* has the flavor of the 19th-century Grand Tour. But they were no wide-eyed sight-seers; they were perceptive, informed, well tailored vagabonds who explored all the colorful byways and remote backwoods of the country and enjoyed all the worldliness of the cities.

Beneath all the flummery of their salad days they were serious, dedicated artists. In this period Barber managed to write the *Overture to the School for Scandal*, *Music for a Scene from Shelley*, the Cello Sonata, *Dover Beach*, and some of his now well-known songs. And they quickly learned how to mix business with pleasure and made international connections which bore fruit in later years. When the war came they settled in America, and finally at Capricorn in 1943.

As the years passed their lives became more complicated. Menotti's career made him a world traveler; he founded the Spoleto Festival and added opera directorship to his accomplishments. The serious pragmatic Barber could not help but feel a real change slowly undermining their relationship. He was home-oriented, a product of a stable background; Menotti, a member of a large eccentric family, was now an international figure. Barber admitted feeling pangs of jealousy and thought that Menotti was ruined by Spoleto. Barber's nature was not inclined to the theatrical high jinks and turbulent activities of Spoleto which Menotti reveled in. The festival more and more infringed not only on their relationship, but it invaded the privacy of Barber's aristocratic reticence. Menotti has often quite candidly discussed in print their difficulties at this time.

As Menotti's reputation grew his operatic ventures made him a peripatetic world traveller. He was seldom home. Barber was left with the burdens of the day-to-day problems and expenses of Capricorn. When it was sold in 1973 he was the one who was more deeply affected. He had lost his vital center, and never regained another. That Barber was more overwhelmed than Menotti when they finally separated does not mean that Menotti was remote or unfeeling, although his outward cavalier manner seemed to imply this to some of their friends. He had greater resiliency and outside distractions to help him over the rough times. The introspective Barber did not, and he was beset with other problems.

There are no villains in this sad and very human story, and such a friendship can never really be broken. In later years their lifestyles were certainly different, but until the end of Barber's life he and Menotti were indissolubly committed to each other.

During the mid-1960s Barber was wounded by the turn of events [the failure of *Antony and Cleopatra*], but not fatally. He retired for a few years to his chalet in Santa Christina, Italy. Here he reassessed his values and went through a period that could be called his Dark Night of the Soul. When he recouped his strength he returned to America and revised *Antony and Cleopatra*.

Barber's music of the 1970s, with the exception of *The Lovers* and the *Third Essay*, was more reflective and contemplative than it had been. But in nothing he wrote — *Fadograph*, the Fischer-Dieskau cycle, the Ballade for piano, and the Canzonetta from his unfinished oboe concerto — does he show any sign of morbidity or unhappiness. These beautifully crafted, resigned pieces are far removed from the funereal and other-worldly pieces Britten and Shostakovitch wrote when they, too, knew they had a limited time to live. The *Third Essay* (1978), his last major work, has all the vigor and imagination of its two companion pieces.

He rented a small New York apartment in the East 60s which had the authentic Barber look — simple but expensive, complete scores of composers from Schütz to the contemporary bound in Moroccan leather, shelves lined with books, a few modern paintings (including some of his temperas), comfortable chairs, a large sofa, a few personal knick-knacks and mementos, some photographs of family and friends, flowers, in short an aura of gracious living. But this was deceptive. He was going through a terrible time, battling depression, loneliness, alcoholism, creative difficulties. It was almost impossible for him to concentrate or be really interested in anything, or anybody.

He was a man of the country and it was heart rending to see him standing on the small terrace of his apartment wistfully looking beyond the highrise across the street. He was very noise conscious and was physically pained by the bustle of the traffic. One of his few consolations was that he liked to hear Benny Goodman, who lived above him, play the clarinet. They became friends.

How he managed to do anything at all during this time is a miracle; it indicates his basic inner strength and a steely refusal to capitulate to the demons within. With the help of his patient and Figaro-like housekeeper Valentin Herranz, he finally managed to be himself again.

Later he moved to an elegant, beautifully furnished apartment on Fifth Avenue facing Central Park. He would make a rueful point of telling you that the park was not country but "a bunch of trees surrounded by noise," and watching people manipulating toy boats on the lake — a fad at the time — was "tiresome and boring." He had always suffered from ennui; he was too intelligent not to. Now it was intensified.

Barber gave himself a party on his 68th birthday. He spent months in planning and preparing for it. That extraordinary evening was a consummate example of Old World formality and Barber's consummate taste and flawless attention to detail. The food and decor were a work of art. All the friends and colleagues he admired and was attached to were invited. The guest list read like a Who's Who of the musical and intellectual world. His look as he surveyed the beautiful room from a raised banquet table was unforgettable — a penetrating sad, resigned awareness; this was his farewell to the world of art that he loved. He knew he had an incurable cancer.

In Barber's last years, he was attended to by Valentin who prepared his meals and saw to his material needs. And Charles Turner, his close friend for many years, at this time of physical and emotional crisis was a constant companion, on call 24 hours a day.

In the final phase of his illness, after he was brought home from a visit to Menotti's estate in Scotland, Barber was surrounded and helped by his innumerable friends. It was not too difficult to love the real Barber.

Even in his very painful last weeks he retained remnants of his ironic wit and sly humor. It popped out unexpectedly. His talent for mimicry and acidity that deflated pomposity never diminished. Nor did his total addiction to Baskin and Robbins Rocky Road chocolate ice cream. His interest in soap opera was constant; he had to be kept informed of the daily activities of the characters in "As the World Turns."

Lying in a hospital bed with an oxygen mask over his face, he never lost his distinguished elegance, sometimes showing flickering signs of humor. Doctors and nurses (around the clock) adored him and were deeply moved when they heard of his death. Menotti had brought him back to his apartment so he could be in familiar surroundings. His life-long friend was there when he passed away on 23 January 1981.

Barber was indeed a complex man. He gave the appearance of being what he really was not. He was a supersophisticate, imperious, ironic, one who did not suffer fools gladly. He had high standards for himself and others. His heart was rarely on display, well concealed under his Roman patrician manner. But his heart was large, his wit hid his sensitivity, his melancholy was his response to the sadness of the world. The taste and refinement of the America that gave us a Samuel Barber is rapidly disappearing — but it is there in his music if we but listen.

Listen, it says, listen.

Once upon a time there was...

Paul Wittke

SAMUEL BARBER (1910–1981)
NOTES ON THE SONGS

Sources: In the notes that follow the sources for all quotations from Samuel Barber's diary and letters are two books by Barbara Heyman, *Samuel Barber: The Composer and His Music* (Oxford University Press, 1992), and *A Comprehensive Thematic Catalog of the Works of Samuel Barber* (consulted in manuscript, publication forthcoming as of this writing in 2010). These two volumes were also principal sources for research. Several other additional sources were consulted, among them: *Samuel Barber: A Guide to Research* by Wayne C. Wentzel (Routledge, 2001); *Samuel Barber Remembered: A Centenary Tribute* edited by Peter Dickinson (University of Rochester Press, 2010); "Samuel Barber: An Improvisatory Portrait," essay by Paul Wittke, published at www.schirmer.com, and various liner notes.

Songs published during the composer's lifetime, in chronological order by year of publication

THREE SONGS, Op. 2

These are Barber's first published songs, published by G. Schirmer in 1936. In a 1978 WQXR radio interview Barber stated, "I went to them [G. Schirmer] and I think I took twelve songs in and they turned down nine. They were right." The twelve songs submitted to Schirmer were presumably composed between c. 1927 and 1934. Even though the three songs were not written as a set, they were published as such, and given the designation of Op. 2. Rose Bampton, a Curtis classmate of Barber's who later sang at the Metropolitan Opera, most likely gave the first performance of the Op. 2 songs as a set in London in June, 1935 at the home of Viscount (Waldorf Astor) and Viscountess Astor.

The Daisies
words by James Stephens

Composed on July 26, 1927. The song was dedicated to Daisy Barber, the composer's mother. (Her proper name was Marguerite McLeod Beatty Barber.) The original composition (see Appendix) features an alternate introduction from the published edition, among other differences. The punctuation in the present edition, which differs from the original edition, has been made after consulting the published poem.

Barber was greatly encouraged by his uncle, composer Sidney Homer, and aunt, Louise Homer, a contralto who sang at the Metropolitan Opera. At times young Sam stayed with the couple at their summer home near Lake George, New York. It was there that he composed "The Daisies," at Roger's Rock, a club on the lake. Sidney Homer had set poetry by Irish poet and novelist James Stephens, and may have interested Sam in Stephens' work. Barber's attention to Stephens may also have been due to the author's collected poems, released in the U.S. in the fall of 1926. Additionally, Stephens made nine tours of the U.S. between 1925 and 1935, and thus was in the American public consciousness.

In Barber's diary, documented by scholar Barbara Heyman, the composer made this entry on September 9, 1927: "A whole morning at Aunt L's studio. She…worked like a dog on my songs which made me feel cruel (to have to waste her glorious voice on them at all.) 'Shame' and 'The Daisies' and 'Dance' she did to perfection." A few days later, on September 15, 1927, Barber's diary entry reads:

> My last day at Rogers Park, and Bill Pullman and I sat down by the lake, for the last time, and talked it over. All I can say is that I thank God for it, and the only way I can thank Him is to give it back in my songs, and that I have tried to do. 'Evening' [An Evening Falls], 'Dance,' 'Daisies,' 'Shame,' 'Piper,' 'The End of the Road,' and 'Watcher' — they are all my experiences and emotions this summer, translated into music — and 'Dance' particularly stands for the summer in general.

All seven songs on Barber's list of compositions from the summer of 1927 were settings of poetry by James Stephens. Only "The Daisies" survived; the remaining manuscripts were either later destroyed or lost. With the gentle guidance of his composer uncle, and the devoted interest of his singer aunt, the summer of 1927 was clearly a happy time of growth for the composer.

Louise Homer included her nephew's songs on recital tours, and possibly sang "The Daisies" in her 1927 recitals. Barber sang the song in performances in Philadelphia in 1934, and in Rome in 1936. In the recorded 1953 performance by Leontyne Price, soprano, and Samuel Barber, piano, the pronoun "she" in m. 20 was changed to "he." We can conclude from this that the composer has then given license for a female singer to adjust the pronoun in this way.

With rue my heart is laden
words by A.E. Housman

Composed on June 30, 1927. Dedicated to Gama Gilbert, a close friend while the composer was a student at Curtis. No manuscript exists from the initial composition. Barber later recopied, edited and apparently transposed the song for two manuscripts, both dated January 25, 1928. On one he indicates that the original key of composition was C minor, though both these manuscripts are in B minor. The song's introduction was added in revision; the original introduction was briefer. Long phrases were in Barber's manuscript, restored in the present edition; they were omitted by the Schirmer editor in the original edition. With an arrow to the first piano phrase marking, Barber writes, "Kindly mark slurs on proof very plainly." In what appears to be a Schirmer editor's handwriting the choices for Low Voice and High Voice key are cited at the end of the manuscript, in preparation for publication. The editor offers the original key as the Low Voice key, which Barber approved, and offered two choices as the High Voice transposition, D minor and E minor. Barber circled the vocal range for D minor and added the words "high key OK."

British poet A.E. Housman (1859-1936) wrote the 63 poems of *A Shropshire Lad* in the 1880s, and after several rejections from publishers finally published it himself in 1896. Poems from the cycle appealed to composers as early as 1904, with a setting by Arthur Somervell. Other composers followed, including Ralph Vaughan Williams, George Butterworth, Ivor Novello, John Ireland, and Michael Head. By the time of Barber's setting "With rue my heart is laden" was one of the most famous of the poems from *A Shropshire Lad*. This poem and others from the set gained heightened meaning during and after the unprecedented human loss of World War I. Indeed, "With rue my heart is laden" easily could have been written about that devastating war.

Bessie Bobtail
words by James Stephens

Composition was completed in August, 1934, in Camden, Maine. Dedicated to John and Edith Braun, friends with whom Barber had stayed in Vienna in the winter of 1934; the Brauns also owned a home in Maine, and had invited Barber for a visit there. Barber studied lieder singing with John Braun; Edith Braun was a pianist and composer. The song title is the same as Stephens' poem title. Barber called this a "narrative song," modeled after character driven, dramatic lieder. Barber himself sang the first known performance, at the New Century Club, Philadelphia, October 23, 1934, along with "The Daisies" and "There's nae lark."

There were far more pre-publication changes and edits on Barber's early published works than on later ones, understandable as the young composer was learning the craft and art of having his work published. Barber's manuscript has a dotted half note on the downbeat of m. 39, which would mean two quarter rests before the quarter note at the end of the bar. This was changed by the Schirmer editor to a whole note followed by one quarter rest before the quarter note. Barber approved the proof and saw the change, so we assume that this was his final intention.

The work of Irish poet James Stephens had been favored by Barber since 1927, when he made seven settings. ("The Daisies" is the only one of the 1927 Stephens songs to have survived; the other six are lost.) Barber directed that the words in the final section of the song be italicized, though this is not the case in the published poem. However, we have used the punctuation of the published poem rather than the punctuation in the original edition of the song.

THREE SONGS, Op. 10

Published by G. Schirmer, 1939. Unlike the songs of Op. 2, which were not written as a set, Barber composed what was designated as Op. 10 as "Three Songs to poems from 'Chamber Music' by James Joyce," according to the manuscript title page. The set as ultimately published was not as originally composed. In 1935, when living in Rome, Barber went through an enthusiastic period of discovery of James Joyce, along with two friends who shared the same enthusiasm, Dario Cecchi and his sister Susanna. Between November 17 and December 5 of 1935 Barber composed four James Joyce songs: "Of that so sweet imprisonment," "Rain has fallen," "Sleep now," and "Strings in the earth and air." Another Joyce setting, "I hear an army," was completed in July of 1936. A sixth followed in 1937, "In the dark pinewood." From these six James Joyce songs, Barber apparently chose the three published as Op. 10 in 1939; one can only speculate at his reasoning for the choices.

Chamber Music, a collection of 36 poems by James Joyce (1882-1941), was published in 1907, and was among the earliest works of the great Irish modernist writer. Two years after the collection was published Joyce wrote to his wife, Nora, after she had discovered *Chamber Music*:

> I like to think of you reading my verses (though it took you five years to find them out). When I wrote them I was a strange lonely boy, walking about by myself at night and thinking that some day a girl would love me. But I never could speak to the girls I used to meet at houses. Their false manners checked me at once. Then you came to me. You were not in a sense the girl for whom I had dreamed and written the verses you find now so enchanting. She was perhaps (as I saw her in my imagination) a girl fashioned into a curious grave beauty by the culture of

The original manuscript with the abbreviated introduction, later extended

generations before her, the woman for whom I wrote poems like 'Gentle lady' or 'Thou leanest to the shell of night.' But then I saw that the beauty of your soul outshone that of my verses. There was something in you higher than anything I had put into them. And for this reason the book of verses is for you. It holds the desire of my youth and you, darling, were the fulfillment of that desire.

Rain has fallen
words by James Joyce

Composition was completed on November 21, 1935, at the American Academy, Rome. Dedicated to Dario Cecchi. Barber sang the first known performance on April 22, 1936 at the American Academy, Rome, and accompanied himself.

Barber's original introduction was only one measure long (the last half of m. 4), later revised. The Joyce untitled poem is usually called by the entire first line, "Rain has fallen all the day," number 23 of the 36 poems in *Chamber Music*. The breath comma in measure 27 also appears in the first manuscript source.

Sleep now
words by James Joyce

Composition was completed on November 29, 1935, at the American Academy, Rome. Dedicated to Susanna Cecchi. Barber sang the first known performance on April 22, 1936 at the American Academy, Rome, and accompanied himself.

The poem is number 24 of the 36 poems in Chamber Music.

Joyce's original lines are:

> O sleep, for the winter
> Is crying "Sleep no more."

Barber repeated "sleep no more" twice.

I hear an army
words by James Joyce

Composition was completed on July 13, 1936, at St. Wolfgang, Austria. The poem is the last of 36 poems in Joyce's *Chamber Music*. Mezzo-soprano Rose Bampton gave the first performance, with Barber at the piano, at the Curtis Institute of Music, Philadelphia, on March 7, 1937. Barber later made a voice and orchestra version of the song.

FOUR SONGS, Op. 13

Published by G. Schirmer, 1941. The first performance of the complete set occurred on April 4, 1941, at Curtis Institute of Music, Philadelphia; Barbara Troxell, soprano; Eugene Bossart, piano. This opus is a loose grouping of diverse poets and subjects. It is unclear whether Barber wrote the songs as a set, or if their grouping as Op. 13 was a practical publishing choice.

A Nun Takes the Veil
Heaven-Haven
words by Gerard Manley Hopkins

Composed 1937. Hopkins' poem title is: "Heaven-Haven: A Nun Takes the Veil." Dedicated to English cellist Rohini Coomara, who shared Barber's interest in Hopkins' poetry. Barber later made an arrangement of the song for unaccompanied four-part chorus. The subject matter of the poem foreshadows *Hermit Songs*.

Oxford educated British poet Gerard Manley Hopkins (1844-1889) converted to Roman Catholicism in 1868, and destroyed most of his poetry. He would not write again for seven years. "Heaven-Haven" is one of the few early poems that survived. Hopkins became a Jesuit priest, and later a professor of Greek literature at University College Dublin. His poetry, largely unpublished during his lifetime, became valued in the twentieth century for its innovations in freedom of prosody and imagery, unusual in the Victorian era.

The Secrets of the Old
words by William Butler Yeats

Composition was completed in September, 1938. One assumes that the *con ped.* section ends in m. 40, though this is not indicated.

The Irish poet and playwright William Butler Yeats (1865-1939) was one of the major literary figures of the early twentieth century. The poem title is the same as used with the song, and is the ninth of eleven poems in the set *A Man Young and Old*, published in Yeats' 1928 book of poetry, *The Tower*.

Sure on this shining night
words by James Agee

Composition was completed in September, 1938. Dedicated to Barber's sister, Sara. Measure 20 is a 4/4 bar in the manuscript, and also a 4/4 bar in Barber's orchestrated version of the song. Barber may have changed it to 3/4 on proofs.

The tie from the lowest note in m. 8 to m. 9 does not appear in the manuscript; it may have been added on proof. There are two manuscript sources. The final bars of the piano part differ in each from the published version. Barber apparently made revisions on proofs before publication. In the earlier manuscript the final four measures appear as:

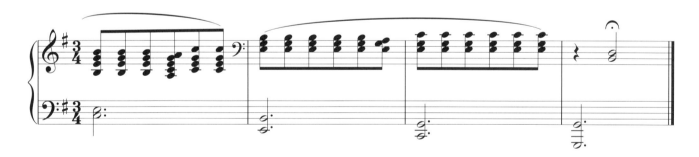

In the second manuscript, the final four measures appear as:

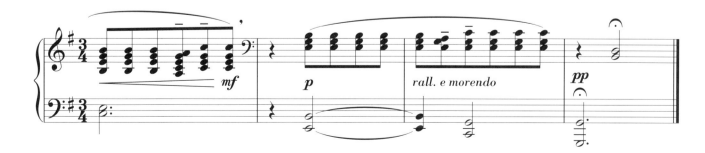

This has become the most famous of Barber songs. He later created a voice and orchestra version, and also a choral arrangement. The composer told an anecdote about a 1979 conversation with a New York City telephone operator who asked him to sing the beginning of "Sure on this shining night" to prove that he was Samuel Barber.

Though Barber and James Agee would become friends after the composer's setting of *Knoxville: Summer of 1915*, they had not yet met when "Sure on this shining night" was composed. The poem is from the "Descriptions of Elysium" section of the 1934 Agee collection *Permit Me Voyage*. James Agee (1909-1955) was a screenwriter (*The African Queen*), journalist, novelist, and a literate and respected film critic, writing for *Time* and *The Nation*. His movie reviews were later collected in *Agee on Film*. His 1941 book *Let Us Now Praise Famous Men: Three Tenant Families* is considered a masterwork. His posthumously published novel, *A Death in the Family*, won the Pulitzer Prize.

Nocturne
words by Frederic Prokosch

Composition was completed February 11, 1940. As is the case with many Barber songs, the composer added and changed details of dynamics and tempo on the proofs, details not in the manuscript. The piano pedaling indications are Barber's throughout. Barber later made a voice and orchestra version of the song.

American writer Frederic Prokosch (1906-1989) and Barber were friends. Prokosch achieved success in the 1930s with two popular novels, followed by eleven more. He published six collections of poetry, including *The Carnival* (1938), where "Nocturne" appears. In her biography of Barber, Barbara Heyman quotes from a letter by Barber to poet Katherine Garrison Chapin about "Nocturne," where the composer states that he was "not very keen" about the poem, but "the music just popped out for it."

TWO SONGS, Op. 18

Published by G. Schirmer, 1944. The songs were first performed, as a set, by soprano Povla Frijsh and pianist Celius Dougherty at Town Hall, New York City, on February 22, 1944.

The queen's face on the summery coin
words by Robert Horan

Composed in November, 1942. Barber made adjustments on the proofs, which differ in details from manuscripts, though not in note content. Poet Robert Horan (b. 1922) was a friend of the composer, and lived at the house in Mount Kisco, New York, shared by Barber and Gian Carlo Menotti for a time in the 1940s. The poem set by Barber in this song was published in the 1948 collection A Beginning, though it was written in years before. In 1946 Barber wrote a recommendation for Horan to the Committee on Grants for Literature of the National Institute of Arts and Letters: "I consider him… extraordinarily talented. Indeed I have seen no lyric poetry of such caliber since the first poems of Auden and Spender." Horan's *A Beginning* is dedicated to Barber and Gian Carlo Menotti.

Monks and Raisins
words by José Garcia Villa

Composed on February 21, 1943. In the original manuscript the tempo is Moderato, changed on proofs. Barber also orchestrated the song.

Filipino poet José Garcia Villa (1908-1997) attended university in the U.S., and remained there for the rest of his life. Early writings were of prose, but he turned to poetry and devoted most of the rest of his career to the genre. His writing style was innovative and modernist. "Monks and Raisins" was published in the 1942 collection *Have Come, Am Here*. Subsequently, after 1949, Villa developed a "comma style" in poetry, where each word was followed by a comma, which he believed gave each word weight and dignity.

Nuvoletta, Op. 25
words by James Joyce

Published by G. Schirmer, 1952. Composition was completed on October 17, 1947. As was usually the case, Barber made changes on proofs regarding musical indications, dynamics, tempo and other such details, not found in the manuscript, before publication. And as is also usually the case, these pre-publication changes did not change the note content of the manuscript. Piano fingerings and pedaling indications are Barber's. Barber omitted a few words in Joyce's text, shown in brackets below:

> …and she smiled over herself [like the beauty of] the image of the pose of the daughter of the [queen of the] Emperour of Irelande…

The composer chose to repeat Joyce's words "Ah dew!"

Barber composed the song a few months after writing *Knoxville: Summer of 1915*. Eleanor Steber was working with the composer for the forthcoming premiere during the time he composed "Nuvoletta." It is believed that Eleanor Steber gave the first performance of "Nuvoletta," though the date and location are not known.

The words come from James Joyce's comic novel *Finnegans Wake*, written over seventeen years and published in 1939, the great Irish author's last work. The avant-garde book was revolutionary in its idiosyncratic language, including many invented and combined words, and in its nonlinear treatment of characters and plot. Though universally critically acclaimed as a twentieth century masterwork, many readers have found the book impenetrable. Joyce abstractly based his work on a comic Irish music hall song of the 1850s, "Finnegan's Wake."

The plot of the book is impossible to summarize. Nuvoletta (a.k.a. Isabel or Issy), the daughter of Humphrey Chimpden Earwicker and Anna Livia Plurabelle, enacts death scenes at different points. The words to Barber's "Nuvoletta" are just such a section. Barber was as perplexed about some of the text as many singers have been. In a 1978 interview, the composer stated: "What can you do when you get lines like 'Nuvoletta reflected for the last time on her little long life, and she made up all her myriads of drifting minds in one. She cancelled all her engagements. She climbed over the bannistars; she gave a chilly, childly, cloudy cry,' except to set them instinctively, as abstract music, almost as a vocalise."

Many will find instructive the 1953 live performance recording by Leontyne Price, with the composer at the piano.

MÉLODIES PASSAGÈRES, Op. 27
words by Rainer Maria Rilke

Published by G. Schirmer, 1952. Francis Poulenc famously partnered in recital for over 25 years with French baritone Pierre Bernac. The cycle is dedicated to them. The pair gave the first performance on January 21, 1952 at Dumbarton Oaks, Washington, D.C., followed by performances in Paris and New York in February, 1952. Bernac and Poulenc recorded the cycle that same year, with Barber as page turner in the recording session, but the recording was not released until 1978.

In a 1978 WQXR radio interview with Robert Sherman Barber discussed the cycle:

> The text of *Mélodies passagères* is by Rainer Maria Rilke. He wrote it in French because he was at that time the secretary of Rodin in Paris. I was a little bit hesitant about writing in French—although I know French—but setting French to music is ticklish. The French are very, very particular about it. On the other hand, I felt "why not," so I plunged in and did these *Mélodies passagères*… Do you know the real reason that I wrote that in French? It was because I was in love in Paris. How can you not be in love in Paris?

In the same interview Barber discussed Poulenc:

> Poulenc was a good friend, one of my only composer friends, I would say. He dedicated a piece to me and I dedicated these songs to him. He was a wonderful combination of a *boulevardier*—a very worldly Frenchman—and also religious. He sent me down to a place called Rocamadour, which I thought was just dreadful. It was in a ravine someplace where he had had a large statue in silver put in the chapel. He was very, very serious about his religion. No fooling there. You hear that in the music.

In October of 1949 American conductor William Strickland asked Barber to write a song cycle to be performed by Eileen Farrell to be sung at Dumbarton Oaks in the spring of 1950. Barber was busy with other projects, and declined the request for a choral work, but composed three of the songs of what was eventually *Mélodies passagères*, and performed them with Eileen Farrell on April 1, 1950. The first three composed, for that occasion, were "Puisque tout passe," "Le clocher chante" and "Départ." The remaining two songs were written in April of 1951, after he had recently returned from a visit to Paris. This must have been the reference in the 1978 interview confession about being in love in Paris. Additionally, Poulenc and Bernac had asked Barber to extend the cycle, as they felt it was too brief.

The French poetry inspired various aspects of French style in Barber's music, though the composer claimed that he did not try for a "French tone."

Rainer Maria Rilke (1875-1926) was one of the greatest of writers in the German language. His work embodies a transition between traditional nineteenth century poetry and modernism, but he also lived in Paris for several years, and wrote about 400 poems in French. "Puisque tout passe," "Un cygne" and "Départ" come from the Rilke collection *Poèmes français*, published posthumously in 1935. Rilke's "Tombeau" (Barber extended the poem's title) was part of *Tendres Impôts à la France* (Affectionate Duties to France), written from September 1923 to February 1924, but unpublished during the poet's lifetime. After 1921 Rilke moved to the Valais region of Switzerland, resulting in *Les Quatrain Valaisans*, where "Le clocher chante" appears.

Translations by Louise Varése

The translations, which are not literal but instead poetic, were created by Louise Varése, wife of the composer Edgar Varése, for the 1952 Schirmer edition, though the translator was not credited in that original publication nor in the later *Collected Songs*.

Puisque tout passe	*Since all things pass*
Puisque tout passe,	*Since all things pass,*
faisons la mélodie passagère;	*let's make a passing melody;*
celle qui nous désaltère	*the one to quench our thirst*
aura de nous raison.	*will be the one to win us.*
Chantons ce qui nous quitte	*What leaves us, let us sing*
avec amour et art;	*with love and art;*
soyons plus vite	*and swifter let us be*
que le rapide depart.	*than the swift departure.*

Un cygne	*A Swan*
Un cygne avance sur l'eau	*A swan moves over the water*
tout entouré de luimême,	*surrounded by itself,*
comme un glisant tableau;	*like a painting that glides;*
ainsi à certains instants	*thus, at times,*
un etre que l'on aime	*a being one loves*
est tout un espace mouvant.	*is a whole moving space.*
Il se rapproche, double,	*And draws near, doubled,*
comme ce cygne qui nage,	*like the moving swan,*
sur notre âme trouble…	*on our troubled soul…*
qui à cet etre ajoute	*which to that being adds*
la tremblante image	*the trembling image*
de bonheur et de doute.	*of happiness and doubt.*

Tombeau dans un parc	*Grave in a Park*
Dors au fond de l'allée,	*At the end of the avenue, sleep,*
tendre enfant, sous la dalle,	*tender child, beneath the stone;*
on fera le chant de lété	*around your interval we'll sing*
autour de ton intervalle.	*the song of summer.*
Si une blanche colombe	*If a white dove*
Passait au vollahaut,	*flies overhead,*
je n'offrirais à ton tombeau	*I will lay upon your grave*
que son ombre qui tombe.	*Only its shadow that falls.*

Le clocher chante	*The Bell Tower Sings*
Mieux qu'une tour profane,	*Better warmed than a secular tower,*
je me chauffe pour mûrir mon carillon.	*To ripen my carillon am I.*
Qu'il soit doux, qu'il soit bon	*May it be sweet, may it be good*
aux Valaisannes.	*for the girls of Valais.*
Chaque dimanche, ton par ton,	*Every Sunday, tone by tone,*
je leur jette ma manne;	*I throw them out my manna;*
qu'il soit bon, mon carillon,	*may it be good, my carillon,*
aux Valaisannes.	*for the girls of Valais.*
Qu'il soit doux, qu'il soit bon;	*May it be sweet, may it be good;*

samedi soir dans les channes	*into their beers on Saturday nights,*
tombe en gouttes mon carillon	*drop by drop, falls my carillon*
aux Valaisans des Valaisannes.	*for the boys and the girls of Valais.*

Départ	*Departure*
Mon amie, il faut que je parte.	*My sweet, I must go away.*
Voulez-vous voir	*Would you like to see*
l'endroit sur la carte?	*the place on the map?*
C'est un point noir.	*It's a black point.*
En moi, si la chose	*In me, it will be*
bien me réussit,	*if the thing succeeds,*
ce sera un point rose	*a rose-red point*
dans un vert pays.	*in a green land.*

HERMIT SONGS, Op. 29

Published by G. Schirmer, 1954. Composed November 1952 to February 1953. The cycle was commissioned by the Elizabeth Sprague Coolidge Foundation, to be performed on the occasion of the Annual Founder's Day Concert. Elizabeth Sprague Coolidge (1864-1953) was an heiress and music lover whose foundation was, in part, devoted to the encouragement of chamber music, especially championing contemporary composers. The illustrious list of composers who benefitted from the Coolidge Foundation included Bartók, Bloch, Britten, Copland, Hindemith, Martinů, Milhaud, Poulenc, Prokofiev, Respighi, Ravel, Schoenberg and Stravinsky. She donated funds to the Library of Congress for its Coolidge Auditorium. *Hermit Songs* was premiered there by soprano Leontyne Price and Barber on October 30, 1953, just five days before Elizabeth Coolidge's death.

As composition began in November 1952, Barber wrote to his composer uncle, Sidney Homer:

> I have come across some poems of the 10th century, translated into modern English by various people, and am making a song cycle of them, to be called, perhaps "Hermit Songs." These were extraordinary men, monks or hermits or what not, and they wrote these little poems on the corners of MSS they were illuminating or just copying. I find them very direct, unspoiled and often curiously contemporaneous in feeling.

In the same letter Barber wrote out the texts of the songs. After the last (the song which was later titled "The Desire for Hermitage"), Barber wrote:

> Dear Uncle, do not take the last one literally; I am not that much of a Hermit, for I have just rented a little apartment in New York, having decided that there is some life in the old dog yet.

The original G. Schirmer edition of *Hermit Songs* included the following introduction, written by Barber:

> The *Hermit Songs*, commissioned by the Elizabeth Sprague Coolidge Foundation, were first performed by Leontyne Price, soprano, with the composer at the piano, at the Library of Congress, Washington, D.C., on October 30, 1953. They are settings of anonymous Irish texts of the eighth to thirteenth centuries written by monks and scholars, often on the margins of the manuscripts they were copying or illuminating — perhaps not always meant to be seen by their Father Superiors. They are small poems, thoughts or observations, some very short, and speak in straightforward, droll, and often surprisingly modern terms of the simple life these men led, close to nature, to animals and to God. Some are literal translations and others, where existing translations seemed inadequate, were especially made by W.H. Auden and Chester Kallman.

Robin Flower in *The Irish Tradition* has written as follows: "It was not only that these scribes and anchorites lived by the destiny of their dedication in an environment of wood and sea; it was because they brought into that environment an eye washed miraculously clear by a continual spiritual exercise that they, first in Europe, had that strange vision of natural things in an almost unnatural purity."

The published introduction to the original edition continues with a quotation from *Stories from Keating's History of Ireland*, edited by Osborn Bergin, a passage chosen by Barber:

Mochua and Clumcille lived at the same time and Mochua, being a hermit in the waste, had no worldly goods but only a cock, a mouse and a fly. And the office of the cock was to keep the hour of matins for him. As for the mouse it would never suffer him to sleep but five hours, day and night, and if he was like to sleep longer, being weary with vigils and prostrations, the mouse would fall to licking his ear till it woke him. And the fly's office was to be walking along each line of his psalter as he read it, and when he was weary with singing his psalms, the fly would abide upon the line where he left off until he could return again to the saying of the psalms. Now it came to pass that these three precious ones died soon. And upon that Mochua wrote a letter to Columcille in Alba, sorrowing for the death of his flock. Columcille replied to him and this is what he said: "My brother," he said, "marvel not that they flock should have died, for misfortune ever waits upon wealth."

Solitude and aloneness were a theme of Barber's life and work. He craved silence and solitude for composition, and preferred the country to the city. The separated individual appears in various meaning and contexts in other Barber works beyond *Hermit Songs*: "With rue my heart is laden," "Bessie Bobtail," "A Nun Takes the Veil," "Sure on this shining night," "Despite and Still" and "Solitary Hotel." James Agee's text for *Knoxville: Summer of 1915* is certainly about an individual's inevitable aloneness, though not in actual solitude. And in the opera *Vanessa*, the title character's seclusion is related to the same theme.

Barber's Irish heritage steered him to Irish poetry as early as the 1920s, and Irish literature remained an interest, though he had not traveled to Ireland. In the summer of 1952 Barber made a trip to Donegal, where he delighted in reading Yeats. The composer discovered that Yeats' grave was surrounded by tombstones of Barbers, possibly his unknown distant relatives. The choice of medieval Irish texts for *Hermit Songs* certainly seems related to the Irish trip a few months before composition.

The songs were not actually composed for Leontyne Price. In a letter of May, 1953 he describes the completed songs and adds, "but haven't found the ideal singer yet." Price was a student of Florence Page Kimball, a friend of Barber's. Barber and Menotti heard Price in Kimball's studio in May or June of 1953 in an informal recital of her students. Price's rise to fame was still ahead of her, and she had never sung a professional recital. Barber gave Price the cycle to learn, but still floundered about the choice of singer. In a letter of July 24, 1953 to William Strickland Barber writes:

Do you know the soprano [Irmgard] Seefried? I have sent her my Hermit Songs to look over; they are to be sung by someone in October at the Library of Congress. I do not know whether Seefried is the right one or not, I love her singing but have never met her and do not know how good her English is. She is supposed to be a delightful person. Maybe you would meet her and play them with her, although I am sure she is very busy with the Salzburg season. The negro soprano, Leontyne Price—very talented—is learning them here and I shall hear them next week. Do you know the baritone Fischer-Dieskau?

It is interesting to note that Barber's concept for the premiere of *Hermit Songs* was not necessarily for soprano, indicated by his interest in Dietrich Fischer-Dieskau (for whom he would later write a set of songs). Barber was not opposed to transpositions of his songs, even for first performances. Eleanor Steber was apparently considered briefly for *Hermit Songs*, but Price obviously impressed Barber. She must have sung the cycle that August in her teacher's studio for him. The composer William Schuman, Barber's exact contemporary and then the president of the Juilliard School, recalled in a 1981 interview:

> I was at the first performance of the *Hermit Songs* given by Leontyne Price at the home of her teacher Florence Page Kimball with Barber at the piano. That was one of the great experiences I recall of hearing new music.

By the end of the summer Barber had written of Price, "she does them beautifully; it is a beautiful voice." Price and Barber collaborated closely after *Hermit Songs*, and remained friends until his death. He composed the opera *Antony and Cleopatra* for her, and the cycle *Despite and Still*. Price very frequently performed Barber songs on her many recitals. Other Barber songs were performed by Price and Barber at the Library of Congress premiere of *Hermit Songs*, including "The Daisies," "Nocturne," "Sleep Now" and "Nuvoletta."

Price and Barber were invited to perform *Hermit Songs* at the Twentieth-Century Music Conference in Rome in April, 1954. In liner notes to the compilation recording "Modern American Vocal Works," which includes *Hermit Songs*, Ned Rorem wrote of his personal memories of the performance:

> In the Roman spring of 1954, for a fortnight we attended concert after charmless concert of the dead-serious and absurdly complex efforts of Boulez's acolytes. How Samuel Barber came to be invited is anyone's guess. Yet suddenly one Tuesday, when we had grown bug-eyed at the gravity of it all, onto the stage came Sam to accompany the unknown Leontyne Price, every inch a diva with her azure sequins, in Hermit Songs. From the first bars of "At Saint Patrick's Purgatory" the all-knowing audience exchanged glances: you don't compose trash like this anymore. Still, the glamorous dynamism of Leontyne was hard to scorn — nothing like it had ever been experienced on land or sea. But when the hit song "The Monk and His Cat" came round there were audible hisses, and the close of the cycle brought loud boos mixed with furtive cheers. Yet who today recalls the other programs? While the Hermit Songs prevail. Separately and as a group they are perfection, being technically what singers like to wrap their tongues around, and emotionally both broad and precise.

Price made her New York recital debut in November, 1954, again singing *Hermit Songs*, with Barber at the piano. Alvin Ailey choreographed a 1961 solo ballet to the cycle, which he danced himself.

At Saint Patrick's Purgatory
words 13th century Gaelic, anonymous, translated by Sean O'Faolain

Composed on November 17, 1952.

Church Bell at Night
words 12th century Gaelic, anonymous, translated by Howard Mumford Jones

Composed on November 3, 1952.

St. Ita's Vision
words attributed to Saint Ita, 8th century Gaelic, translated by Chester Kallman

Composed on January 9, 1953.

The Heavenly Banquet
words attributed to St. Brigid, 10th century Gaelic, translated by Sean O'Faolain

Composed on November 13, 1952.

The Crucifixion
words 12th century anonymous Gaelic from *The Speckled Book*, translated by Howard Mumford Jones

Composed on October 26, 1952.

Sea-Snatch
words 8th or 9th century Gaelic, anonymous, translated by Kenneth Jackson

Composed on January 6, 1953.

Promiscuity
words 9th century Gaelic, anonymous, translated by Kenneth Jackson

Composed on January 15, 1953.

The Monk and His Cat
words 8th or 9th century Gaelic, anonymous, translated by W.H. Auden

Composed on February 16, 1953. Dedicated to Isabelle Vengerova, a gift for her seventy-sixth birthday. Vengerova was Barber's piano teacher at Curtis. A legendary presence there, her students included Leonard Bernstein, Lukas Foss, Leonard Pennario, Gary Graffman and Abbey Simon. Barber adapted the song for SATB chorus and piano.

The Praises of God
words 11th century Gaelic, anonymous, translated by W.H. Auden

Composed on January 27, 1953. Dedicated to the memory of Mary Evans Scott.

The Desire for Hermitage

words 8th or 9th century Gaelic, anonymous, translated by Sean O'Faolain, altered by S.B.

Composed on January 15, 1953.

DESPITE AND STILL, Op. 41

Published by G. Schirmer, 1969. Composition began in June, 1968 and was completed on August 14, 1968, taking place at Barber's rural house at Santa Cristina, Italy. The cycle was written for Leontyne Price and dedicated to her. First performed by soprano Leontyne Price and pianist David Garvey on April 27, 1969 at Avery Fisher Hall, New York.

Barber had been commissioned to write *Antony and Cleopatra* for the Metropolitan Opera for the occasion of the opening of the new opera house at Lincoln Center. The premiere drew the intense attention of critics and the media. Many technical problems plagued the production, and it was regarded as a failure. Barber retreated to Italy and was in semi-seclusion for some time following the opera's premiere. Some who knew

To my friend Leontyne Price

1. A Last Song */

Robert Graves

* In the original "A Last Poem"

him have said that he never recovered his confidence after the failure of *Antony and Cleopatra* in 1966. Barber wrote very little in the two years after the opera's premiere. *Despite and Still* was the only lengthy work composed in the late 1960s. Only a few other small compositions were written in this period of Barber's life.

Though the relationship between the texts chosen or their theme is not obvious, the songs are deeply personal compositions, possibly composed for no reason other than the composer's need to express himself after a dry spell. Barber admitted that the music is more dissonant in this cycle at times than his typical style.

A Last Song
words by Robert Graves

The song was composed in June, 1968. Graves' poem is titled "A Last Poem," changed by Barber. Barber considered different keys for Leontyne Price, and prepared manuscripts in more than one key for rehearsals.

British writer Robert Graves (1895-1985) was a poet, novelist and translator. He gained notoriety for his personal poetry about the horrors of World War I, his translations and re-interpretations of Greek myths, and his historical novels, such as *I, Claudius*.

My Lizard (Wish for a Young Love)
words by Theodore Roethke

Composed on July 20, 1968. American poet Theodore Roethke (1908-1963) won the 1954 Pulitzer Prize for the poetry collection *The Waking*. Barber probably encountered this poem in the *Collected Poems of Roethke*, published in 1966. Roethke titled his poem "Wish for a young wife," which Barber altered in his subtitle.

In the Wilderness
words by Robert Graves

Composed on August 3, 1968. See "A Last Song" for comments on Graves.

Solitary Hotel
words by James Joyce, from *Ulysses*

Composed on August, 1968. The brief text is excerpted from Joyce's modernist masterwork novel, *Ulysses*, which was published in magazine installments from 1918 to 1920, then in its entirety as a book in 1922.

Despite and Still
words by Robert Graves

Composed on August 14, 1968.

THREE SONGS, Op. 45

Published by G. Schirmer, 1974. Composition was completed by the end of August, 1972, at Barber's house in Santa Cristina, Italy. Commissioned for baritone Dietrich Fischer-Dieskau by the Lincoln Center Chamber Music Society. First performed by Fischer-Dieskau and pianist Charles Wadsworth on April 30, 1974, Alice Tully Hall, New York City.

The Three Songs, Op. 45 were composed in 1972 during a period of restlessness and personal uncertainty, with the pending sale of the Capricorn house in Mount Kisco, New York, that Barber and Menotti had shared. The composer wrote to a friend:

> I have finished three songs for Fischer-Dieskau and sent them to the copyist in New York. Worked rather hard on them, too. One is a translation from Georg Heym, one (a funny one) trans. from the Polish. Now he can get to work on them, F.D., I mean. They are for New York in January. You must get his beautiful record of Schumann's *Dichterliebe*.

Fischer-Dieskau postponed the January 1973 premiere due to illness. Barber quotes from the singer in a letter to a friend:

> I had the following letter from Fischer-Dieskau, which I transcribe:
>
> "Dear and admired S——B——, it is more than a misfortune to me that a flu had to cross over your beautiful premiere which I was so looking forward to. Let me assure you that I love your songs and certainly will perform them as soon as it is ever possible for me.
>
> Take all my best wishes and the expression of deep regret for my cancellation.

Now have I fed and eaten up the rose
words by James Joyce (from the German of Gottfried Keller)

Composed in Spoleto, Italy, March, 1972. The four measure postlude was not in the original version, added at some point before publication. Gottfried Keller (1819-1890) was a Swiss writer of novels, short stories and lyric poetry. The original German title of this poem is "Da hab' ich gar die Rose aufgegessen" from the 1846 cycle of nineteen poems, *Gedanken eines Lebendig-Begrabenen* (Thoughts of a Living Burial). James Joyce, always fascinated by music and song, made a translation from an abbreviated and altered version of the poem, which was set in song by Othmar Schoek.

The original full length Keller poem appears below:

> Da hab' ich gar die Rose aufgegessen,
> Die man mir in die starre Hand gegeben!
> Daß ich noch einmal Rosen würde essen,
> Ich hab' es nie geahnt in meinem Leben.
>
> Ich möcht' nur wissen, ob es seine weiße,
> Ob eine rothe Rose das gewesen?
> Am letzen Blatt, das spielend ich zerreiße,
> Möcht' ich es fühlend mit den Fingern lesen.
>
> Wie vielen Gärten voller Knospenprangen
> Bin ich gedankenlos vorbeigezogen!
> Voll Geigen hat der Himmel mir gehangen—
> Nur fand ich nicht den rechten Fiedelbogen.

Literal translation:

> Since I have even eaten the rose
> The one given to me in the rigid hand!
> That I would once again eat roses,
> I've never dreamed in my life.
>
> I should like to know if it is white,
> Whether a red rose was that?

Barber's original key of composition, later transposed.

On the last page that I tear up easily,
I would like to read it, feeling with his fingers.

How many gardens full of buds splendor
Have I passed by without thinking!
Full violins, the sky hung me —
Only I could not find the right fiddle.

The abbreviated version of the Keller poem, set by Othmar Schoek, translated by Joyce:

Da hab' ich gar die Rose aufgegessen,
Die sie mir in die starre Hand gegeben!
Daß ich noch einmal würde Rosen essen,
Hätt nimmer ich geglaubt in meinem Leben!

Ich möcht' nur wissen, ob es eine rote,
Ob eine weiße Rose das gewesen?
Gib täglich uns, o Herr! von deinem Brote,
Und wenn du willst, erlös' uns von dem Bösen!

Joyce's translation, using his typical style of combined/invented words ("stiffcold," "liveman's"):

Now have I fed and eaten up the rose
Which then she laid within my stiffcold hand.
That I should ever feed upon a rose
I never had believed in liveman's land.

Only I wonder was it white or red
The flower that in the dark my food has been.
Give us, and if Thou give, thy daily bread,
Deliver us from evil, Lord, Amen.

A Green Lowland of Pianos
words by Czeslaw Milosz (from the Polish of Jerzy Harasymowicz)

Jerzy Harasymowicz (1933-1999) wrote more than 40 volumes of poetry. His style often uses invented surrealist mythology. Born in Lithuania, Czeslaw Milosz (1911-2004) was a Polish poet and translator who defected to the U.S. in 1951. His 1953 *The Captive Mind* is a landmark of anti-Stalinism. Milosz received the Nobel Prize in Literature in 1980. This translation of this Harasymowicz's poem was published in *Postwar Polish Poetry*, edited by Czeslaw Milosz.

O boundless, boundless evening
words by Christopher Middleton (from the German of Georg Heym)

Georg Heym (1887-1912) was an expressionist German poet. His rebellious and non-conformist personality is reflected in his writing. He died at a young age after falling through ice while attempting to save a friend when skating. British poet Christopher Middleton (b. 1926) specialized in translating German verse, and became Professor of Germanic Languages at University of Texas, retiring in 1998.

Songs published posthumously, in alphabetical order.

Ask me to rest
words by Edward Hicks Streeter Terry

Composed in July, 1926. First edition, previously unpublished. Terry was a Philadelphia poet. Barber may have encountered the poem in a magazine.

Au claire de la lune
words anonymous (French folksong)

Composed in January, 1926. First edition, previously unpublished. First heard on April 25, 1926 in West Chester, Pennsylvania, performed by mezzo-soprano Lilian McD. Brinton, accompanied by Barber. The song was a result of an assignment for a class taught by Deems Taylor (1885-1966) at Curtis. Even in his teens Barber had begun to master languages, a lifelong interest, and part of his love of Europe. Taylor, a composer and music critic, was a prominent advocate for classical music, serving for years as host of New York Philharmonic radio broadcasts. He was the master of ceremonies in the Disney film *Fantasia*.

Au clair de la lune,	*By moonlight,*
Mon ami Pierrot,	*my friend Pierrot,*
Prête-moi ta plume	*lend me your pen*
pour écrire un mot.	*to write a word.*
Ma chandelle est morte.	*My candle is dead.*
Je n'ai plus de feu.	*I have no more fire.*
Ouvre-moi ta porte	*Open to me your door*
Pour l'amour de Dieu.	*for God's sake.*
Au clair de la lune	*By moonlight*
Pierrot répondit:	*Pierrot replied:*
Je n'ai pas de plume.	*I have no pen.*
Je suis dans mon lit.	*I am in my bed.*
Va chez la voisine.	*Go to the next neighbor.*
Je crois qu'elle y est	*I think it is there*
Car dans sa cuisine	*for in her kitchen*
On bat le briquet.	*it strikes the tender box.*

Beggar's Song
words by William Henry Davies

Composed on January 5, 1936 in Rome while Barber was at the American Academy. First performed by Barber, accompanying himself, on April 22, 1936, American Academy, Rome. Unpublished during the composer's lifetime, the song was published in *Samuel Barber: Ten Early Songs* (G. Schirmer, 1994). Welshman William Henry Davies (1871-1940) was a popular poet in the 1920s. A colorful figure, he spent years as a vagabond in the U.S., documented in his book *The Autobiography of a Supertramp* (1908), but became widely respected after settling in London in 1921. His collected poems were published in 1929.

Ask Me to Rest —

Ask me to rest —— when I can show the world That I have toiled: ——— Then will I heed thy plea; But now — with nothing done — I must go on; I pray, I pray thee ask it not —————— Of ———

Fantasy in Purple
words by Langston Hughes

Composed on September 10, 1925. First edition, previously unpublished. First heard on April 25, 1926 in West Chester, Pennsylvania, performed by mezzo-soprano Lilian McD. Brinton, accompanied by Barber. American writer Langston Hughes (1902-1967) was a major figure of the Harlem Renaissance of the 1920s and '30s. In the mid-1920s Hughes was attending Lincoln University in Chester County, Pennsylvania, where Barber lived. Family friend Robert Kerlin was among the judges for a poetry contest sponsored by *Opportunity: A Journal of Negro Life*. "Fantasy in Purple" was published in the journal. Kerlin likely introduced Barber to Hughes' poem.

In the dark pinewood
words by James Joyce from *Chamber Music*

Composed in 1937 at St. Wolfgang, Austria. Unpublished during the composer's lifetime, the song was published in *Samuel Barber: Ten Early Songs* (G. Schirmer, 1994). See Three Songs, Op. 10 for more information about Barber's settings of Joyce.

La nuit
words by Alfred Meurath

Composed in January, 1925. First edition, previously unpublished. First heard in performance in April, 1926 in West Chester, Pennsylvania, performed by soprano Gertrud K. Schmidt, accompanied by Barber. Even in his teens Barber had begun to master languages, a lifelong interest, and part of his love of Europe.

La nuit c'est l'heure du songe	*The night is the time of thought,*
Des rêves, et de l'amour	*of dreams, and of love,*
De la douleur qui nous ronge,	*from the pain that eats at us,*
Et la fin des maux de ce jour.	*and the end of the ills of the day.*
La nuit c'est le noir et l'ombre,	*The night is black and shadow*
C'est l'heure du doux repos,	*it is the time for soft repose,*
Pour l'homme qui dort dans l'ombre,	*for the man who sleeps in the shade*
Les paupières et le cœur clos.	*the eyelids and the heart closed.*
La nuit c'est le grand silence,	*The night is the great silence*
La solitude et l'ennui;	*the loneliness and boredom;*
Troubles en notre conscience,	*troubles in our conscience,*
Car elle songe la nuit.	*because she thinks in the night.*
Et songe à de tristes choses,	*And think of sad things,*
Car là dans l'ombre est l'abîme!	*for there in the dark is an abyss!*
Heureux l'homme qui repose,	*Blessed is the man who rests*
Et dort dans la nuit sublime.	*and sleeps in the night sublime.*

Love at the Door
words translated by John Addington Symonds from the Greek of Meleager (first century A.D.)

Composed in July, 1934 at the Barber family cottage in the Pocono Mountains of Pennsylvania. Unpublished during the composer's lifetime, the song was published in *Samuel Barber: Ten Early Songs* (G. Schirmer, 1994).

Love's Caution
words by William Henry Davies

Composed on November 7, 1935 in Rome while Barber was at the American Academy. Unpublished during the composer's lifetime, the song was published in *Samuel Barber: Ten Early Songs* (G. Schirmer, 1994). Welshman William Henry Davies (1871-1940) was a popular poet of the 1920s. A colorful figure, he spent years as a vagabond in the U.S., documented in his book *The Autobiography of a Supertramp* (1908), but became widely respected after settling in London in 1921. His collected poems were published in 1929.

Man
words by Humbert Wolfe

Composed on April 1, 1926. First edition, previously unpublished. First heard in performance in April, 1926 in West Chester, Pennsylvania, performed by soprano Gertrud K. Schmidt, accompanied by Barber. Humbert Wolfe (1885-1940) was a widely read British poet of the 1920s. His poetry was set to music by more than one composer, including Gustav Holst's 1929 cycle *12 Humbert Wolfe Settings*.

Mother, I cannot mind my wheel
words by Walter Savage Landor

Composed on February 12, 1927. Published in *Samuel Barber: Ten Selected Songs* (G. Schirmer/Hal Leonard Corporation, 2008). In his diary entry of February 12, 1927 Barber states: "Wrote my new song 'Mother I Cannot Mind My Wheel' in a grand rush — the melody in less than 5 minutes and the acc. in a half hour." British writer and poet Walter Savage Landor (1775-1864) was best known for *Imaginary Conversations*, and the poem "Rose Aylmer."

Music, when soft voices die
words by Percy Bysshe Shelley

Probably composed in August, 1925. Sources exist of two versions of the song. Both have the same vocal melody. The earlier version has an extended piano introduction; there are other differences in the piano part. Barber undoubtedly edited himself and made deliberate changes. We present here the second version of the song. First edition, previously unpublished. First heard on April 25, 1926 in West Chester, Pennsylvania, performed by mezzo-soprano Lilian McD. Brinton, accompanied by Barber. Percy Bysshe Shelley (1792-1822) was a major figure of English romantic poetry, associated with John Keats and Lord Byron. Shelley's second wife was Mary Shelley, author of the novel *Frankenstein*.

Night Wanderers
words by William Henry Davies

Composed on November 1, 1935 in Rome while Barber was at the American Academy. Unpublished during the composer's lifetime, the song was published in *Samuel Barber: Ten Early Songs* (G. Schirmer, 1994). Welshman William Henry Davies (1871-1940) was a popular poet. A colorful figure, he spent years as a vagabond in the U.S., documented in his book *The Autobiography of a Supertramp* (1908), but became widely respected after settling in London in 1921. His collected poems were published in 1929.

Of that so sweet imprisonment
words by James Joyce from *Chamber Music*

Composition was completed on November 17, 1935 in Rome while Barber was at the American Academy. Unpublished during the composer's lifetime, the song was published in *Samuel Barber: Ten Early Songs* (G. Schirmer, 1994). See Three Songs, Op. 10 for more information about Barber's settings of Joyce.

Peace
Words by Paul Elmer More, translated from the Sanskrit of Bhartrhari

Composed on January 5, 1935. First edition, previously unpublished. Indian writer Bhartrhari (or Bhartrihari) (c. 570-651) was a Hindu philosopher and author of the *Śatakatraya*, a work of poetry consisting of three sections of a hundred verses each. In his writings explores vacillation between the pursuits of fleshly desires and those of the spirit.

Serenader
words by George H. Dillon

Composition was completed March, 1934. Composed in Vienna. Unpublished during the composer's lifetime, the song was published in *Samuel Barber: Ten Early Songs* (G. Schirmer, 1994). *Boy in the Wind*, the first collection of poems by American writer George H. Dillon (1906-1968) was published when he was 21. His second book, *The Flowering Stone*, won the Pulitzer Prize.

A Slumber Song of the Madonna
words by Alfred Noyes

Composed in January, 1925. Originally for voice and organ. A voice and piano version followed, which was first heard on April 25, 1926 in West Chester, Pennsylvania, performed by mezzo-soprano Lilian McD. Brinton, accompanied by Barber. Barber's aunt, Louise Homer, sang the song, accompanied by Barber on organ, in 1927. That same year she often sang the voice and piano version of the song on an American recital tour. The song was unpublished during the composer's lifetime, first published in *Ten Early Songs* (G. Schirmer, 1994). British writer Alfred Noyes (1880-1958) produced 60 books of poetry, novels and short stories. He is best known for his narrative poem "The Highwayman."

Stopping by Woods on a Snowy Evening
words by Robert Frost

The date of composition is uncertain. Because of the brand of manuscript paper used, Barber scholar Barbara Heyman speculates that it was composed in late 1935 or early 1936 while Barber was at the American Academy in Rome. First edition, previously unpublished. This is Barber's only setting of the prominent American poet Robert Frost (1874-1963), who often used New England rural life to express broader themes and philosophies. "Stopping by Woods on a Snowy Evening" is his most famous poem, written in 1922 and published in 1923 in the poetry collection *New Hampshire*.

Strings in the earth and air
words by James Joyce from *Chamber Music*

Composed on December 5, 1935 in Rome while Barber was at the American Academy. Unpublished during the composer's lifetime, the song was published in *Samuel Barber: Ten Early Songs* (G. Schirmer, 1994). See Three Songs, Op. 10 for more information about Barber's settings of Joyce.

There's nae lark
words by Algernon Charles Swinburne

Composed on October 29, 1927. Louise Homer may have performed the song in France in 1928. Barber gave the first documented performance, accompanying himself, on October 23, 1934 at New Century Club, West Chester, Pennsylvania. Unpublished during the composer's lifetime, the song was published in *Samuel Barber: Ten Early Songs* (G. Schirmer, 1994). British poet and novelist Algernon Charles Swinburne (1837–1909) invented the roundel form, and contributed to the Eleventh Edition of the *Encyclopaedia Britannica*. He was nominated for the Nobel Prize in Literature each year from 1903 to 1909, but never won.

THREE SONGS: THE WORDS FROM OLD ENGLAND
words from the *Oxford Book of English Verse: 1250-1900*

Lady, when I behold the roses
words anonymous, Old English

Composed in February, 1925. First edition, previously unpublished. First heard on April 25, 1926 in West Chester, Pennsylvania, performed by mezzo-soprano Lilian McD. Brinton, accompanied by Barber.

An Earnest Suit to His Unkind Mistress Not to Forsake Him
words by Sir Thomas Wyatt

Composed on November 16, 1926. First edition, previously unpublished. First heard on November 20, 1926 in West Chester, Pennsylvania, performed by mezzo-soprano Lilian McD. Brinton, accompanied by Barber.

Hey nonny no!
words anonymous, Christ Church manuscript

Composed on November 27, 1926. Dedicated to Aunt Louise Homer. Published in *Samuel Barber: Ten Selected Songs* (G. Schirmer/Hal Leonard Corporation, 2008).

Thy Love
Words by Elizabeth Barrett Browning

Composed April 7, 1926. Dedicated to Barber's aunt, Elizabeth Colwell Beatty. British poet Elizabeth Barrett Browning (1806-1861) was one of the most prominent writers of the Victorian era, and was widely known for her *Sonnets from the Portuguese* (published in 1850), which capture the emotion of her period of courtship with poet Robert Browning, whom she married. She felt the poems too personal to publish. After consulting with her husband she decided to pretend they were not her own writing but rather translations "from the Portuguese."

Barber greatly altered Browning's sonnet in his setting, omitting or changing many words. The original sonnet:

> If thou must love me, let it be for naught
> Except for love's sake only. Do not say,
> "I love her for her smile—her look—her way
> Of speaking gently—for a trick of thought
> That falls in well with mine, and certes brought
> A sense of pleasant ease on such a day."
> For these things in themselves, Beloved, may
> Be changed, or change for thee—and love, so wrought,
> May be unwrought so. Neither love me for
> Thine own dear pity's wiping my cheeks dry—
> A creature might forget to weep, who bore
> Thy comfort long, and lose thy love thereby!
> But love me for love's sake, that evermore
> Thou mayst love on, through love's eternity.

TWO POEMS OF THE WIND
words by Fiona Macleod, pseudonym for William Sharp

First edition, previously unpublished. First heard on April 25, 1926 in West Chester, Pennsylvania, performed by mezzo-soprano Lilian McD. Brinton, accompanied by Barber. Barber's aunt, Louise Homer, sang the songs on June 4, 1927 in West Chester, Pennsylvania. Barber wrote of the performance in his diary: "Never have I heard Aunt Louise sing better…My songs made a hit and Longing had to be repeated. I fear my bows were rather awkward…About 160 people came." Louise Homer, a professional singer at the Metropolitan Opera and a frequent recitalist, may have given further performances of the songs elsewhere in recital.

Scotsman William Sharp (1855-1905) wrote poetry and literary biography, and edited published editions of poetry by Ossian, Walter Scott, Matthew Arnold, Algernon Charles Swinburne and Eugene Lee-Hamilton. After 1883 Sharp also published novels and poetry under the secret pseudonym Fiona Macleod, apparently a decision that allowed him creative freedom, though the deception became a burden.

Little Children of the Wind

Composed on October 13, 1924.

Longing

Composed on October 16, 1924.

TWO SONGS OF YOUTH

First edition, previously unpublished. Both songs were first heard on April 25, 1926 in West Chester, Pennsylvania, performed by mezzo-soprano Lilian McD. Brinton, accompanied by Barber.

Invocation to Youth
words by Laurence Binyon

Composed in August, 1925. British poet, dramatist and scholar Robert Laurence Binyon (1869-1943) is best known for *For the Fallen*.

I never thought that youth would go
words by Jessie B. Rittenhouse

Composed in July, 1925. Jessie B. Rittenhouse (1869-1948) was a prominent American editor and compiler of poetry (*The Little Book of Modern Verse*). She did not include her own poems in the collections she edited.

Watchers
words attributed to Dean Cornwell

Composed on February 20, 1926. First edition, previously unpublished. First heard on April 25, 1926 in West Chester, Pennsylvania, performed by mezzo-soprano Lilian McD. Brinton, accompanied by Barber. Louise Homer, Barber's aunt, sang the song often on recitals of 1926 and 1927. Barber quoted press reviews in his diary in November, 1926:

> Los Angeles and San Francisco — I have kept them all — They say: "Sam Barber's fine 'Watchers,' with its eloquent and continent harmonies." — "It will soon be in print, judging from its reception by the audience, and Louise Homer's singing of it." — "A stark song of the seas" — "A fine dramatic song" — "was forceful with its arresting knock of Fate in the accompaniment."

Louise Homer sang the song at Carnegie Hall on January 29, 1927. Barber attended the performance and wrote about it in his diary:

> The eventful day. Sara and I went over on the 10 o'clock from Philadelphia… After lunch went to concert. Great! Aunt Louise sang my song marvelously, with great feeling and dramatic action, and the audience kept applauding so that she repeated it — the only one on the program that she did over. She sang it even better the second time. The high note was thrilling, and the low notes no less so. (She sobbed in one place —) It was a great success.

Of the performance *The New York Times* said: "Mme. Homer proved how vocal and musical the language really is, how expressive it is, and what a fund of pathos and humor it possesses. Samuel Barber's The Watchers had to be repeated. *The New York Sun* commented: "Samuel Barber's 'Watchers,' a lyric of dramatic content, was repeated…" In his diary Barber quoted a further New York review: "A new song, as yet in manuscript, sung by Mme. Homer stirred the audience to demand a repetition, and it was given. It was Sidney [sic] Barber's 'Watchers.' "

His opinion of the song changed. In the liner notes for *Songs of Samuel Barber* (1978), Phillip Ramey quoted Barber as saying that "Watchers" was not very good, though highly dramatic.

Who carries corn and crown
words by Robert Horan

Composed c. 1942. First edition, previously unpublished. Poet Robert Horan (b. 1922) was a friend of the composer, and lived at the house in Mount Kisco, New York, shared by Barber and Gian Carlo Menotti for a time in the 1940s. The poem was published in 1948 (with some changes) in *A Beginning*, but it was written years earlier. Barber's setting is clearly of an early version of the poem, before publication. In 1946 Barber wrote a recommendation for Horan to the Committee on Grants for Literature of the National Institute of Arts and Letters: "I consider him... extraordinarily talented. Indeed I have seen no lyric poetry of such caliber since the first poems of Auden and Spender." Horan's *A Beginning* is dedicated to Barber and Gian Carlo Menotti.

Manuscript Facsimiles of Early Songs

I Do Not Like Thee, Dr. Fell
from Nursery Rhymes or Mother Goose Rhymes Set to Music

The set of seven songs was composed 1918-22. Dedicated to Barber's sister, Sara. Barber wrote the following description as a preface to the set, dated April 8, 1923: "The mistakes in notation, the harmonical errors, the poor constructions — they have not been omitted. They are as I first wrote them, before I knew the tiresome rules of harmony."

In *A Complete Thematic Catalog of the Works of Samuel Barber*, author Barbara Heyman states:

> "I do not like thee, Dr. Fell," originated as Tom Brown's rebuttal to the disciplinarian Oxford don who threatened Brown (1663-1704) with expulsion unless he could translate an epigram of Martial (1, 33, 1): *Non amo te, Sabidi, nec possum dicere quare; Hoc tantum possum dicere, non amo te.* According to the story, Brown replied without missing a beat: I do not love thee, Dr. Fell, The reason why I cannot tell; But this I know, and know full well, I do not love thee, Dr. Fell. Its earliest use as a nursery rhyme was in 1926.

An Old Song
words by Charles Kingsley

Composed 1921. The original manuscript has not survived. However, Barber recopied the song many years later (date of recopying is unknown). That task indicates in itself a fondness for the song. Barber wrote on the manuscript: "composed a long time ago in 1921, aged eleven."

Der Two Fella Joe
words relayed to the composer by a White Mountain Guide

Composed July 1924 at Camp Wyanoke, Wolfeboro, New Hampsire.

October Mountain Weather
words by Samuel Barber

Composed c. October, 1924. First heard on April 25, 1926 in West Chester, Pennsylvania, performed by soprano Gertrude K. Schmidt, accompanied by Barber.

Richard Walters
Editor

SONGS PUBLISHED DURING THE COMPOSER'S LIFETIME

To Daisy

The Daisies
original key

James Stephens

Samuel Barber
Op. 2, No. 1
1927

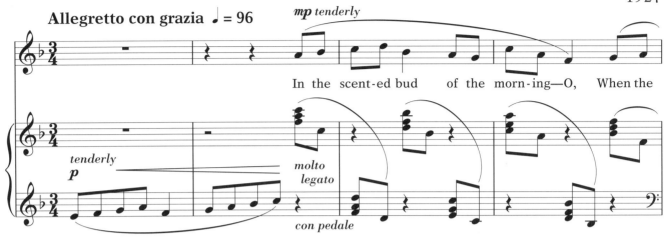

Poem from *Collected Poems of James Stephens.* Printed by permission of The Macmillan Company, publishers.

wan-dered hap-p'ly,★ to and fro; I kissed my dear on ei - ther cheek, In the

bud of the morn - ing— O. A lark sang up from the

breez - y land, A lark sang down from a cloud a - far, As she and

I went hand in hand In the field where the dais - ies are.

★In Stephens' poem the word is "happily," which Barber chose to set on two notes rather than three.

The Windmill,
Rogers Park
July 20, 1927

To Gama Gilbert

With rue my heart is laden

original key: B minor

A. E. Housman

Samuel Barber
Op. 2, No. 2
1927

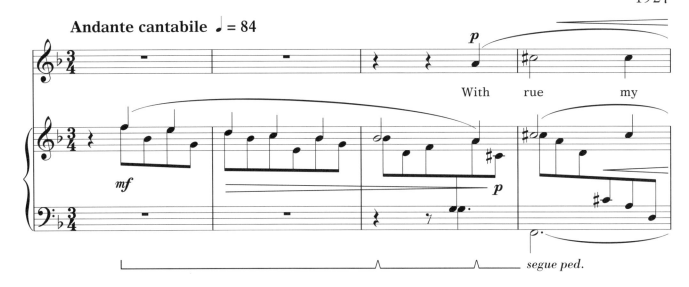

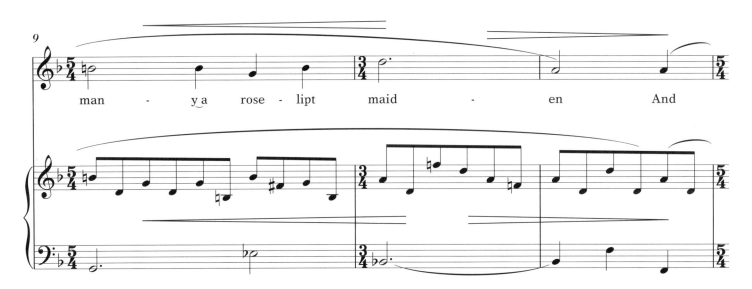

Poem from *A Shropshire Lad*; words used by permission of the poet and The Richards Press Ltd., publishers.

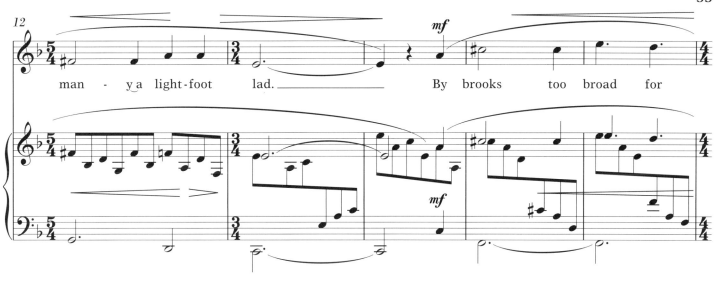

man - y a light-foot lad._____ By brooks too broad for

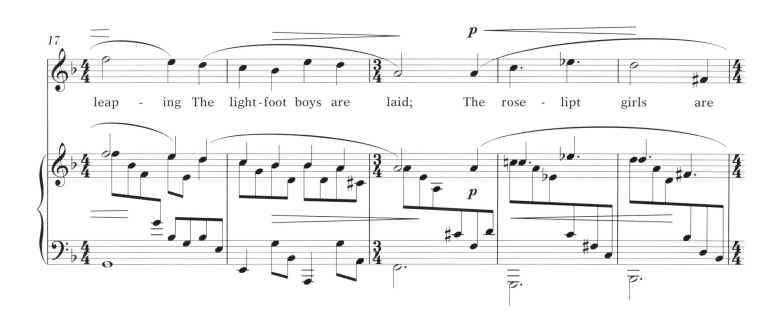

leap - ing The light-foot boys are laid; The rose - lipt girls are

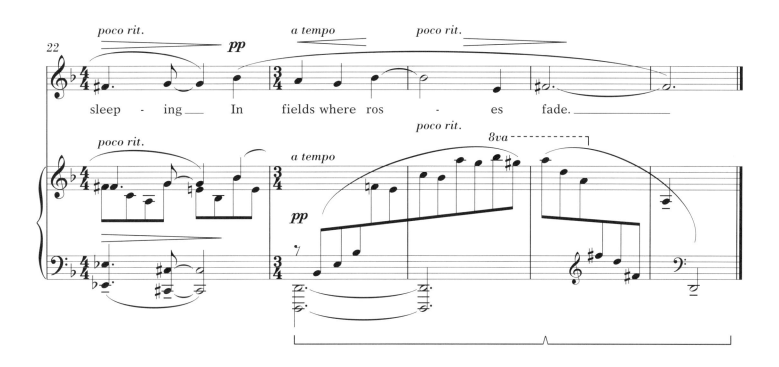

sleep - ing___ In fields where ros - es fade._____

To Edith and John Braun

Bessie Bobtail
original key

James Stephens

Samuel Barber
Op. 2, No. 3
1934

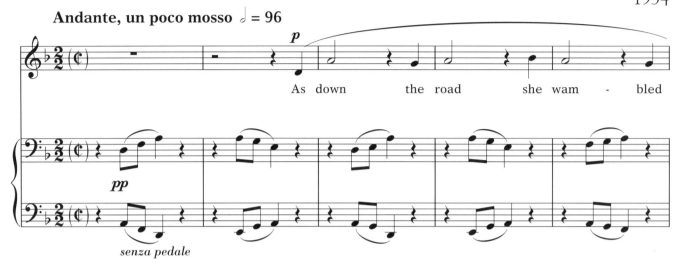

Poem from *Collected Poems of James Stephens*. Printed by permission of The Macmillan Company, publishers.

place at all. She stumped a - long, and wagged her

pate; And said a thing was des - per - ate. Her

face was screwed and wrin-kled tight Just like a nut— and,

left and right, On ei - ther side she wagged her head And

*These optional notes are in Barber's manuscript.

*Barber originally spelled these A-flats as G-sharps in measures 52 and 54, changed on proofs before the first edition.

Camden, Maine
August, 1934

To Dario Cecchi

Rain has fallen
original key: a minor third lower

James Joyce

Samuel Barber
Op. 10, No. 1
1935

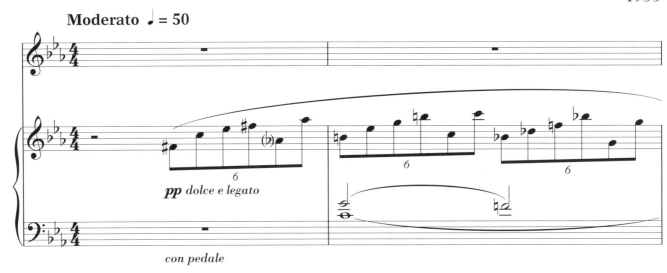

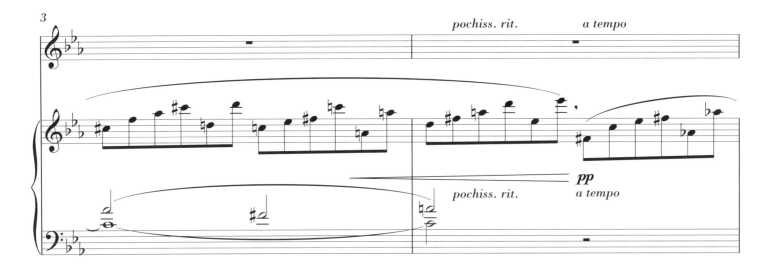

Poem from *Collected Poems* by James Joyce (copyright 1918, 1927, 1936) published by the Viking Press, Inc., New York.

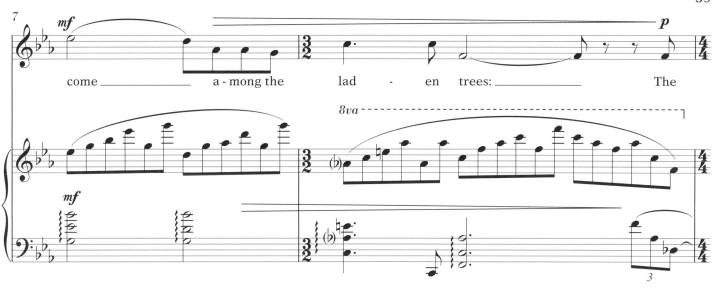

come _____ a - mong the lad - en trees: _____ The

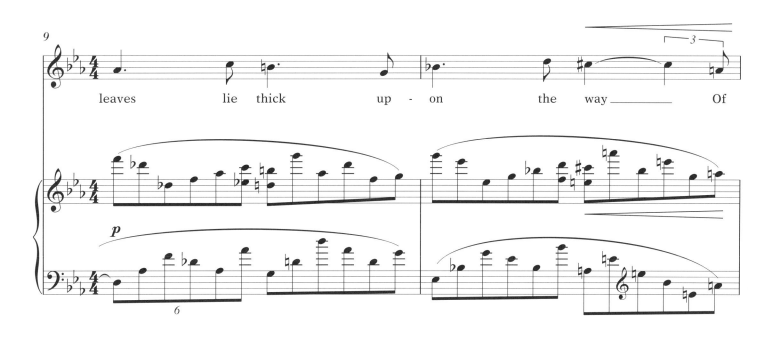

leaves lie thick up - on the way _____ Of

mem - 'ries. _____

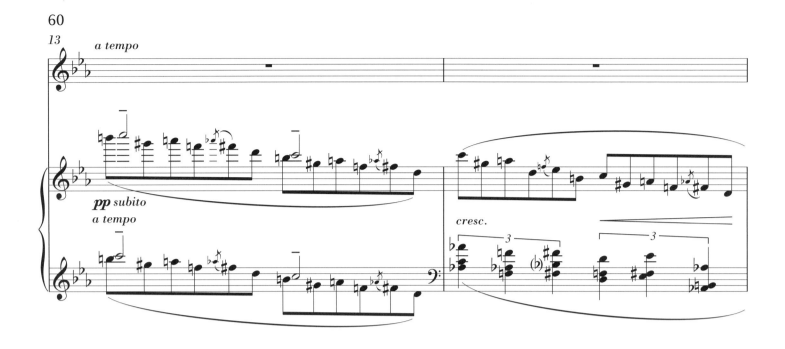

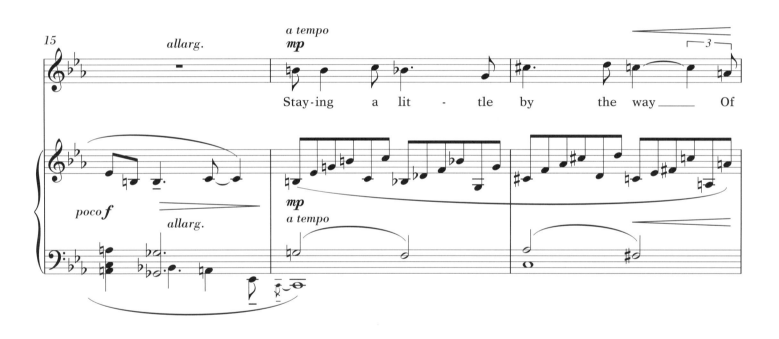

Stay-ing a lit - tle by the way_____ Of

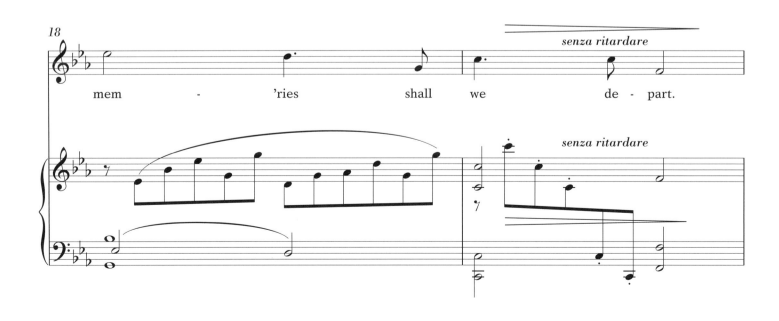

mem - 'ries shall we de - part.

poco a poco più appassionato

Come, _____ my be - lov - ed, where I may

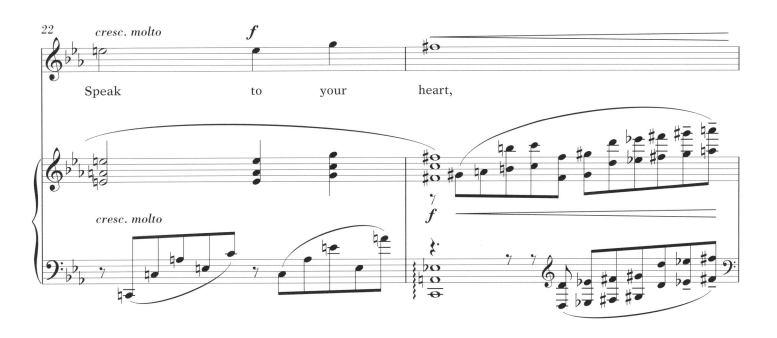

Speak to your heart,

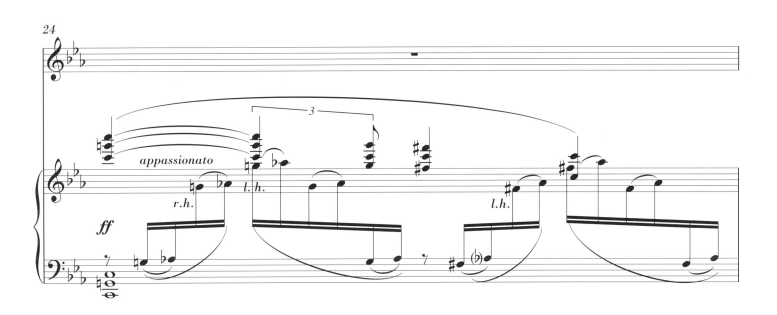

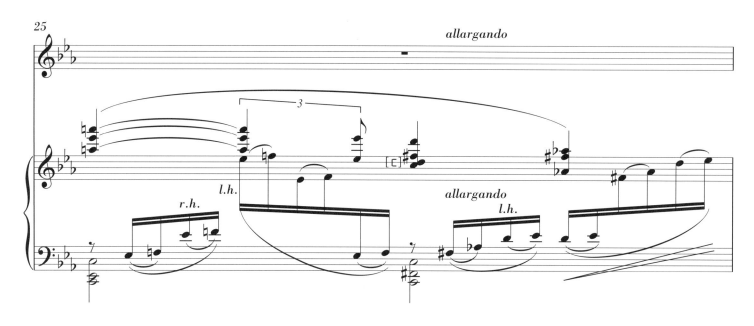

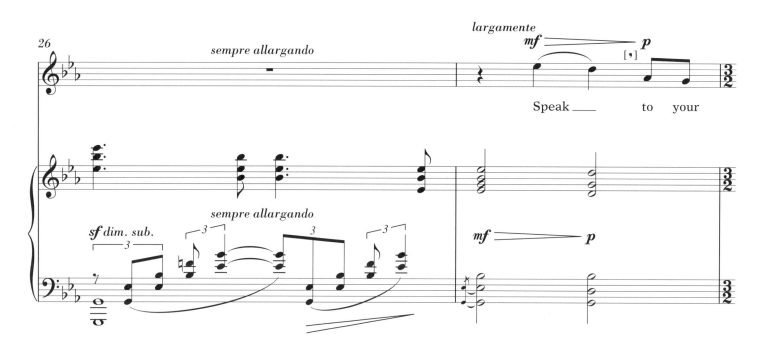

Speak ____ to your

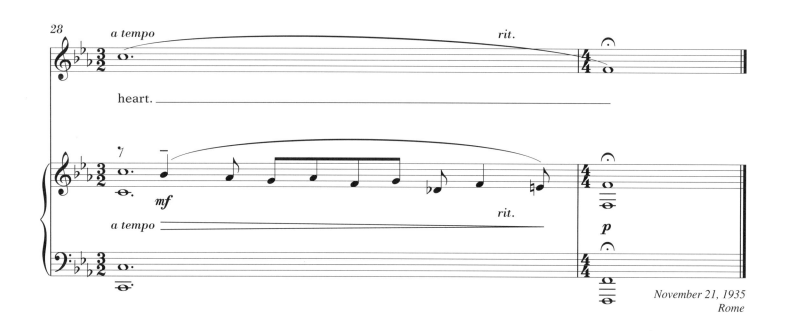

heart. ____

November 21, 1935
Rome

To Susanna Cecchi

Sleep now

original key: a minor third lower

James Joyce

Samuel Barber
Op. 10, No. 2
1935

Sleep now, O sleep now, O you un-qui-et

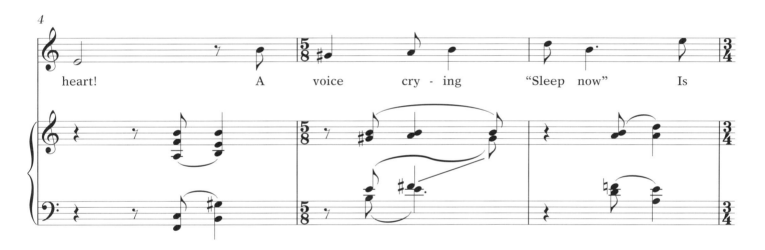

heart! A voice cry-ing "Sleep now" Is

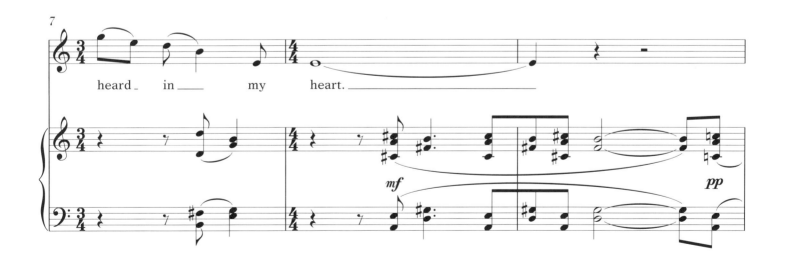

heard in my heart.

Poem from *Collected Poems* by James Joyce (copyright 1918, 1927, 1936) published by the Viking Press, Inc., New York.

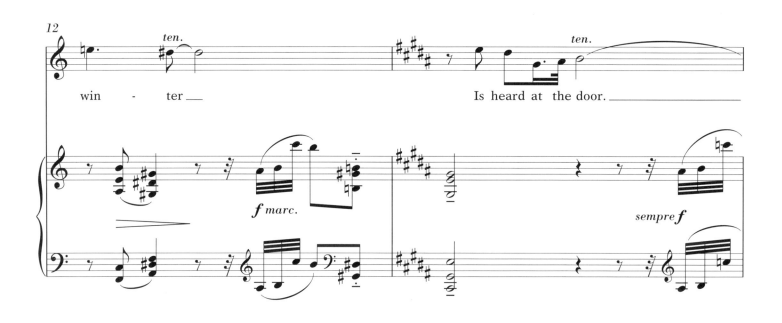

win - ter Is cry - ing "Sleep _____ no _ more, _____

sleep _____ no _ more, _____ sleep no more." _____

Tempo I, tranquillo

My kiss will give peace now And

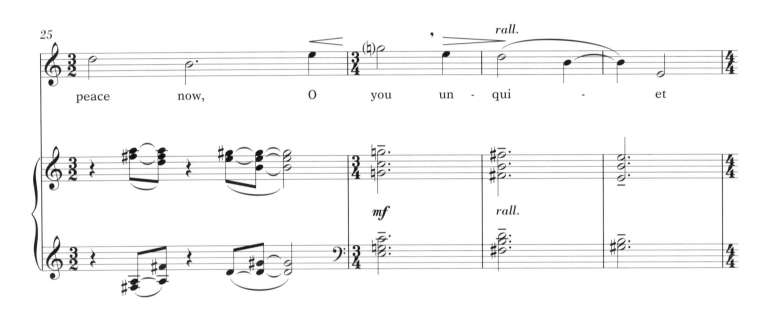

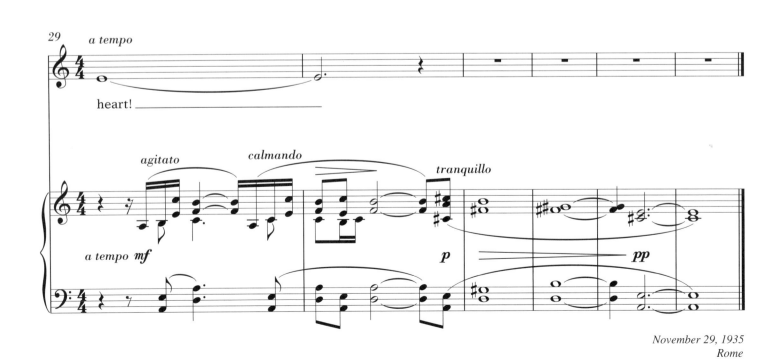

November 29, 1935
Rome

I hear an army

original key

James Joyce

Samuel Barber
Op. 10, No. 3
1936

Poem from *Collected Poems* by James Joyce (copyright 1918, 1927, 1936) published by the Viking Press, Inc., New York.

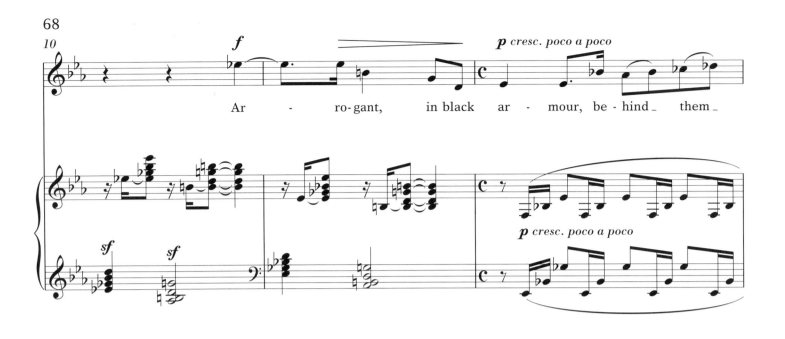

Ar - ro-gant, in black ar - mour, be - hind them stand,

stand, Dis-dain-ing the reins, with flut - t'ring whips, the

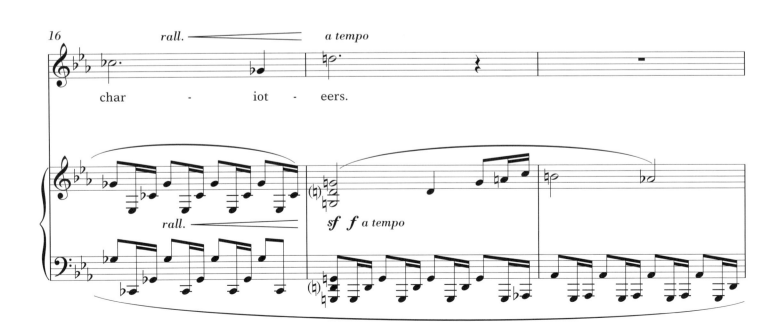

char - iot - eers.

They cry _____ un-to the

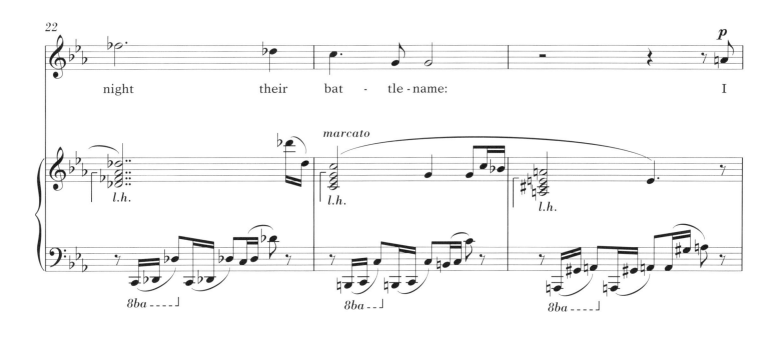

night their bat - tle -name: I

moan in sleep when I hear a - far their whirl - ing laugh - ter.

They cleave the gloom _ of _ dreams, a blind - ing _

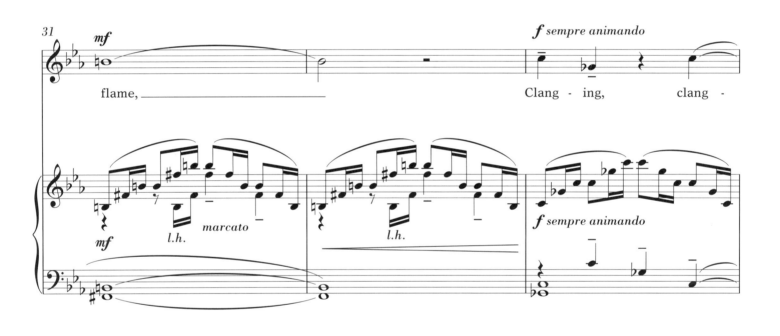

flame,_____ Clang - ing, clang -

- ing up - on the heart_____ as up - on an an - vil.____

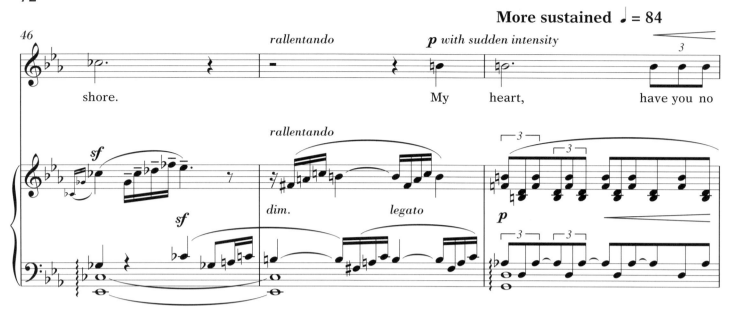

More sustained ♩ = 84

rallentando

p *with sudden intensity*

shore. My heart, have you no

wis - dom thus to de - spair?

f *molto marcato (moving ahead)*

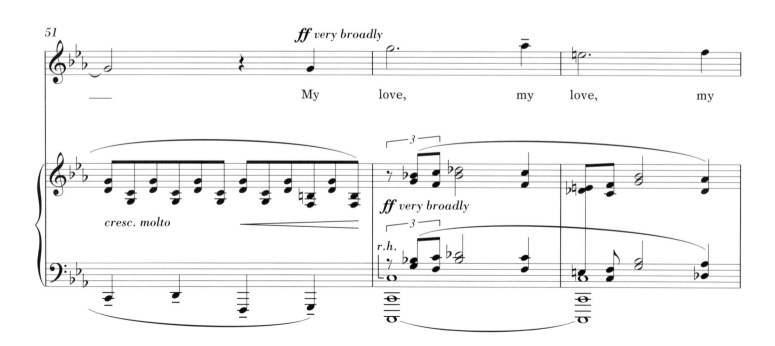

ff *very broadly*

My love, my love, my

cresc. molto

ff *very broadly*

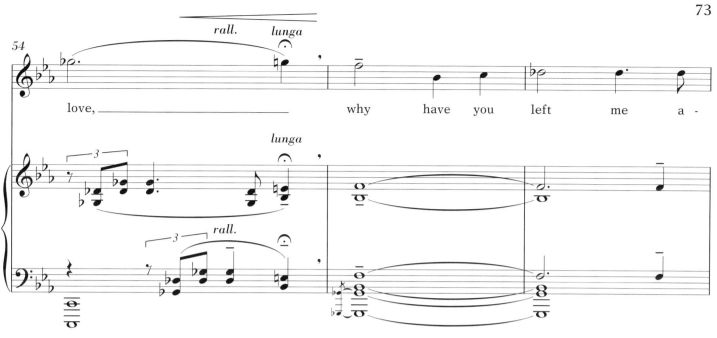

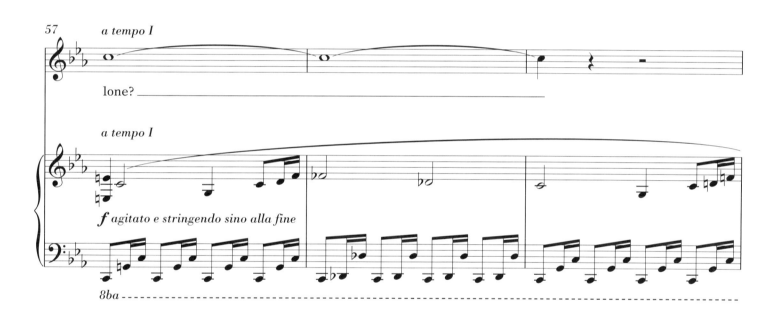

July 13, 1936
St. Wolfgang

To Rohini Coomara

A Nun Takes the Veil

Heaven - Haven

original key: a major third lower

Gerard Manley Hopkins

Samuel Barber
Op. 13, No. 1
1937

Broad and sustained, in exact rhythm ♩ = 48

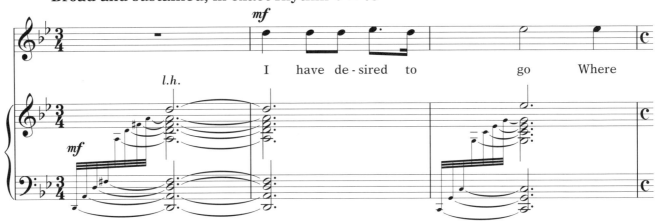

I have de-sired to go Where

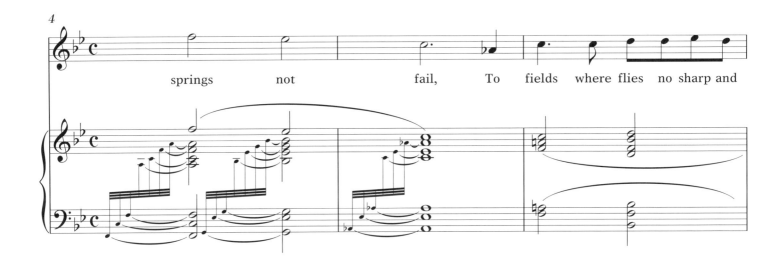

springs not fail, To fields where flies no sharp and

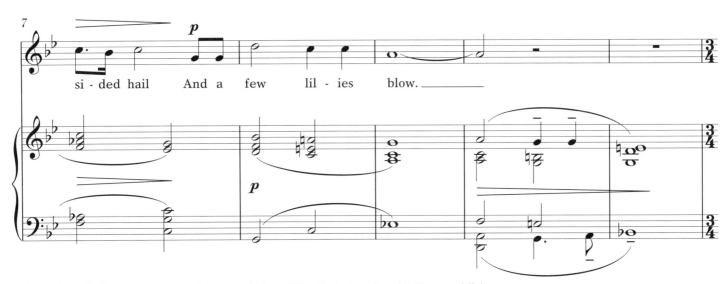

si-ded hail And a few lil-ies blow.

Poem from *Collected Poems*. Used by permission of The Oxford University Press, publishers.

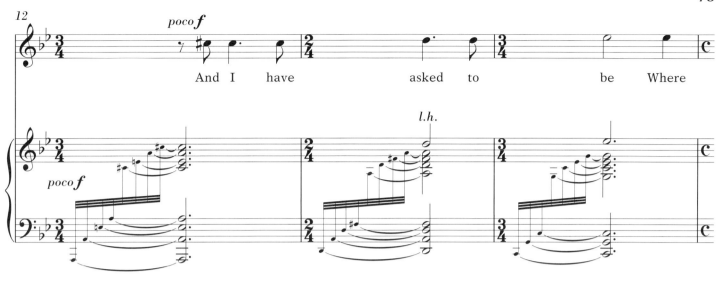

And I have asked to be Where

no storms come, Where the green swell is in the ha - vens dumb,

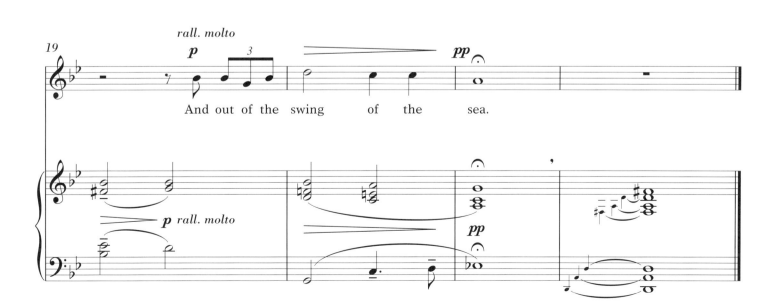

And out of the swing of the sea.

The Secrets of the Old

original key: a minor third lower

William Butler Yeats

Samuel Barber
Op. 13, No. 2
1938

The words of this song are reprinted from *Collected Poems of W. B. Yeats* by permission of Mrs. Yeats and of the Macmillan Company, Publishers.

*"Margery" in Yeats' poem, condensed by Barber to be set on two notes.

September 1938

To Sara

Sure on this shining night

original key: G Major

James Agee

Samuel Barber
Op. 13, No. 3
1938

Text from *Permit Me Voyage*. Used by permission of Yale University Press, Publishers.

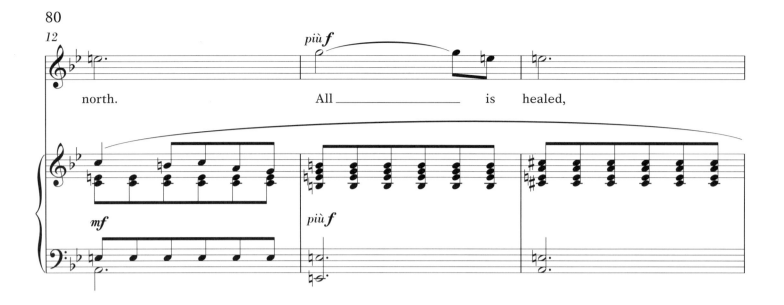

north. All _____ is healed,

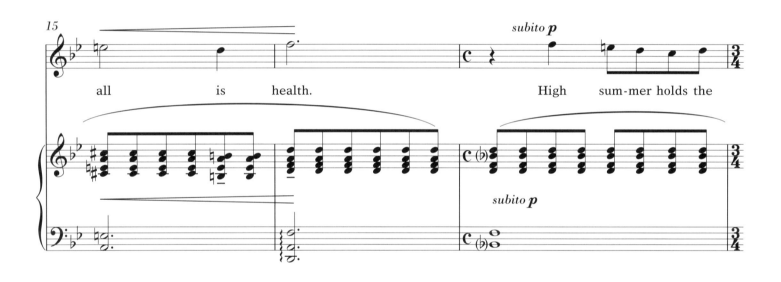

all is health. High sum-mer holds the

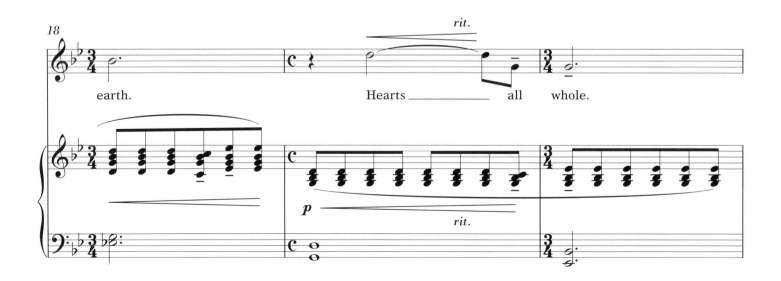

earth. Hearts _____ all whole.

Sure on this shin-ing night I weep for won - der

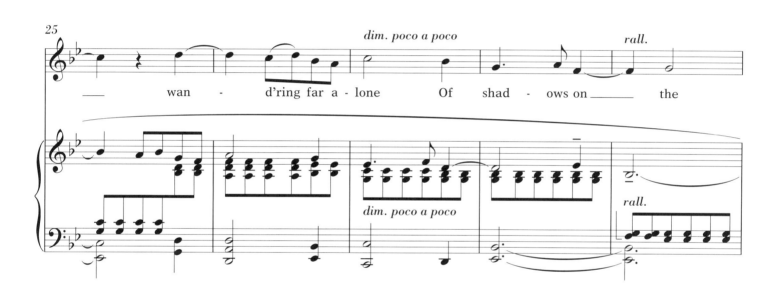

wan - d'ring far a - lone Of shad - ows on the

stars.

September 1938

Nocturne

original key: a major second lower

Frederic Prokosch

Samuel Barber
Op. 13, No. 4
1940

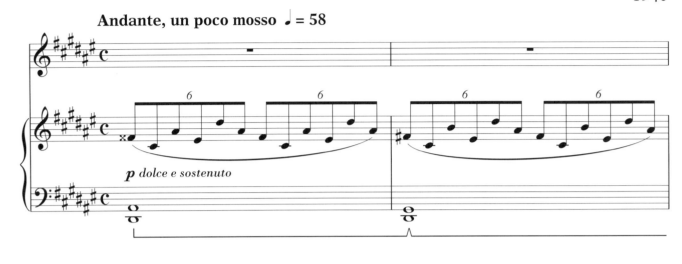

Poem from *The Carnival*. Copyright, 1938, by Harper & Brothers. Printed by special permission of Harper & Brothers and Chatto & Windus.

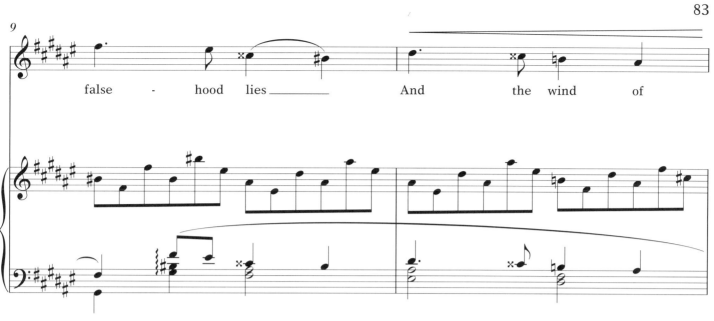

false - hood lies_____ And the wind of

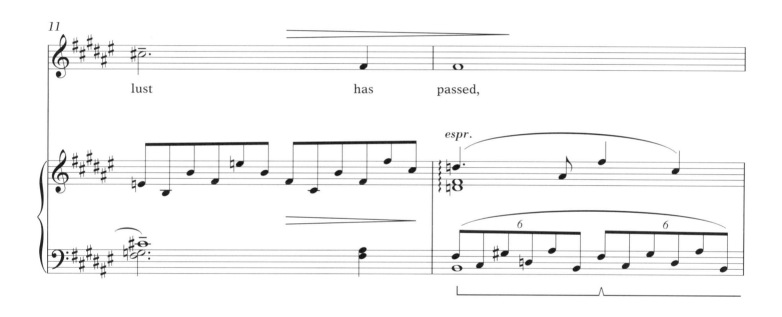

lust has passed,

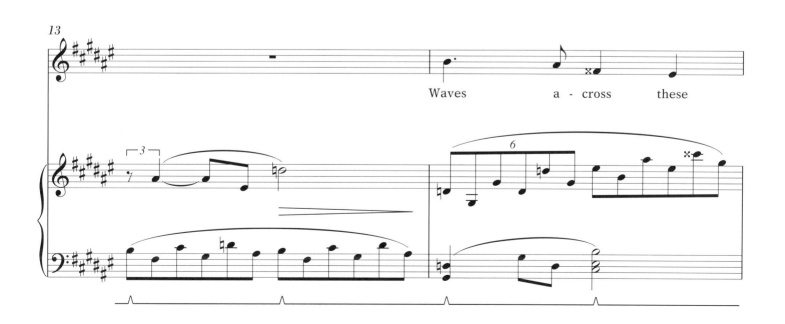

Waves a - cross these

15
hope - less sands   Fill   my heart_____ and end my

17
day,   Un - der-neath   your

19
mov - ing hands   All   my ach - ing

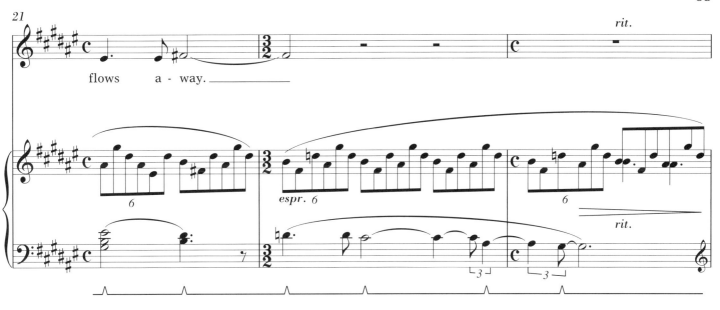

flows a - way.

E - ven the hu - man pyr - a - mids

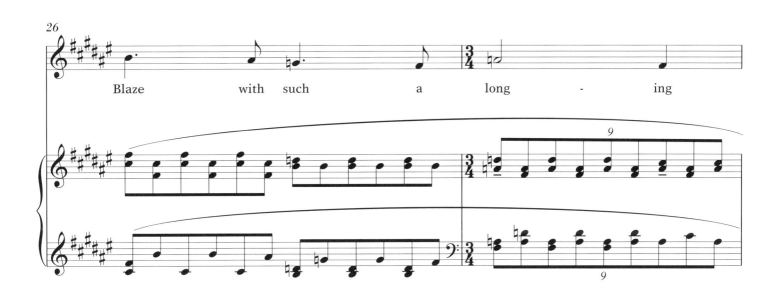

Blaze with such a long - ing

now: _____ Close, my love, your

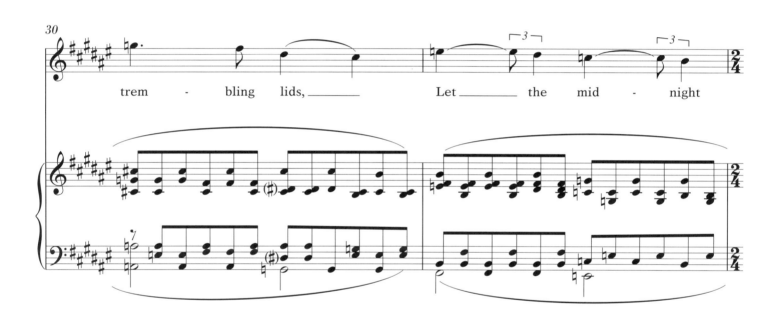

trem - bling lids, _____ Let _____ the mid - night

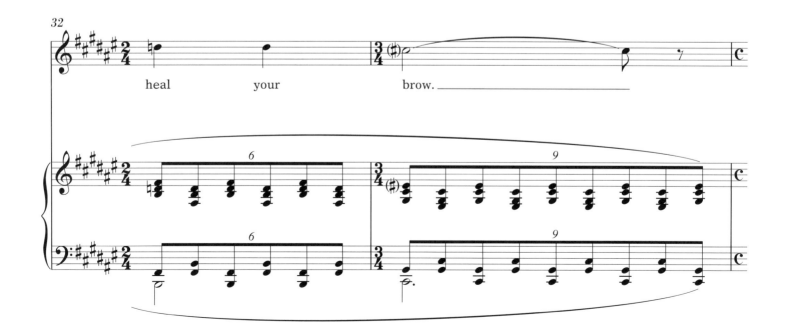

heal your brow. _____

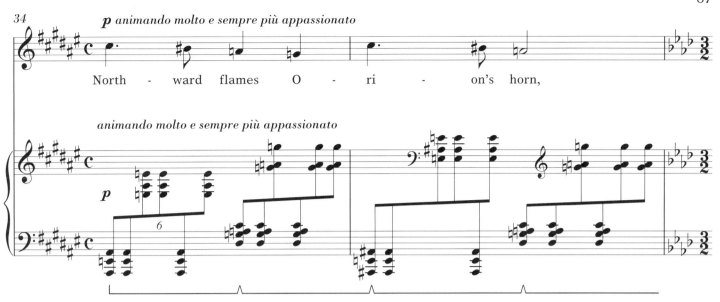

North - ward flames O - ri - on's horn,

West - ward th'E - gyp - tian _ light.

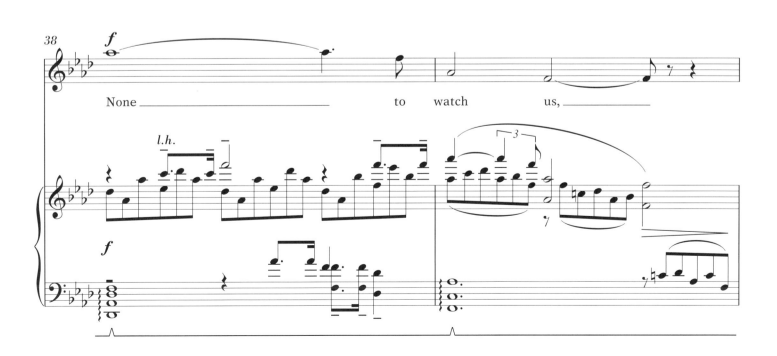

None _____ to watch us, _____

The queen's face on the summery coin

original key

Robert Horan

Samuel Barber
Op. 18, No. 1
1942

walked be - tween_ the stripes_ of rain._____

The birds swing in their *ap - ply ca - ges

and the sol-id sun ___ will walk ___ through straw hous-es where hon-ey ra - ges,

*Horan's published 1948 poem has "appled" here, changed by the poet before publication, after Barber's setting.

churn - ing the light _____ to chalk. _____

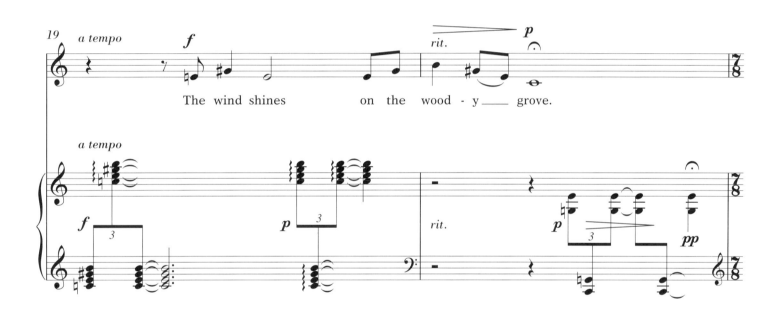

The wind shines on the wood - y _____ grove.

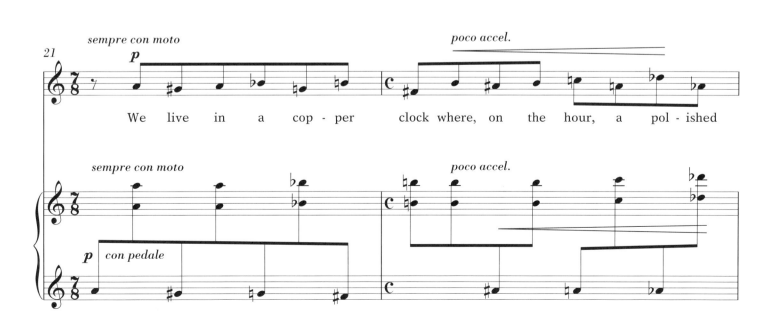

We live in a cop - per clock where, on the hour, a pol - ished

there is too much eye to see all but the near-est dis - or - der.

Tempo I

In the sa - ble shad-ow of this har - bor _____ he lies him

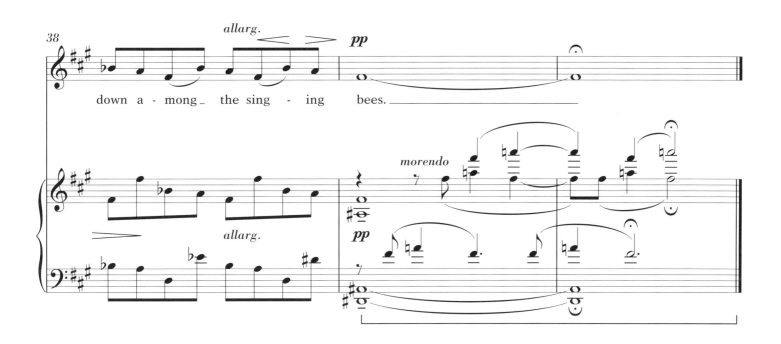

down a - mong_ the sing - ing bees. _____

Monks and Raisins
original key

José Garcia Villa

Samuel Barber
Op. 18, No. 2
1943

I have ob-served pink monks eat-ing blue rai-sins. And I have ob-served blue monks eat-ing pink rai-sins. Stu-dious-ly have I ob-served.

Poem from *Have Come, Am Here*, copyright, 1942, by Viking Press. Used by permission.

Now, this is the way a pink monk eats a blue rai-sin:

Pink is he and it is blue and the pink Swal-lows the blue. __ I swear this is

true. And the way a blue monk eats a

pink rai - sin is this: Blue __ is he and it is

pink_ and the blue   Swal-lows the pink.

And this al - so is truth._____

In-deed I   have ob-served   and my-self par - tak - en   Of blue and pink

rai - sins.　　But　my　joy　was　dif - f'rent:_____

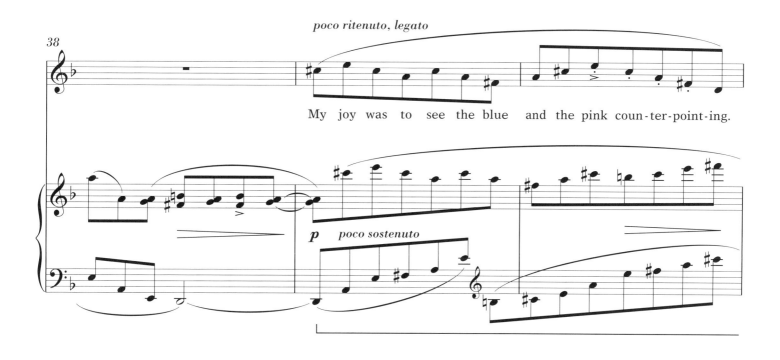

poco ritenuto, legato

My　joy　was　to　see　the　blue　　and　the　pink　coun-ter-point-ing.

p　*poco sostenuto*

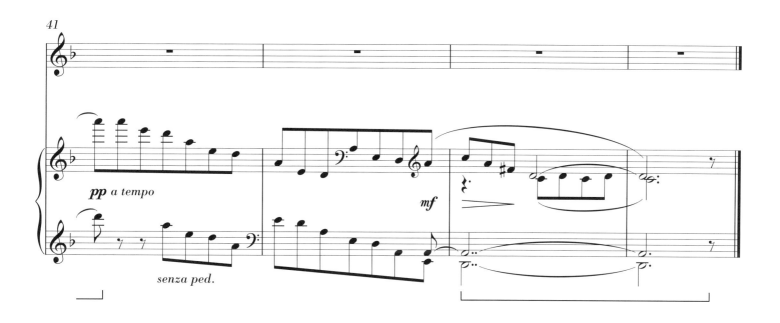

pp a tempo

senza ped.

Nuvoletta
original key

James Joyce
Finnegans Wake

Samuel Barber
Op. 25
1947

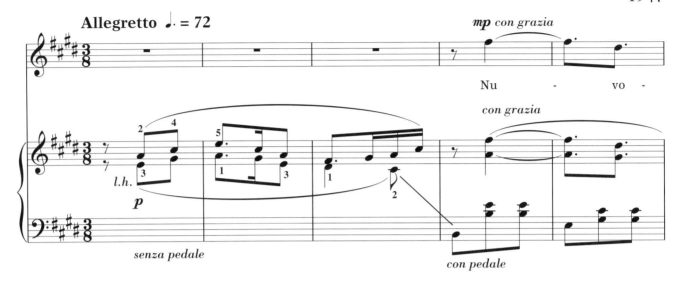

Words copyright 1939 by James Joyce. By permission of The Viking Press, Inc., New York.

self _____ like the im - age of _____ the pose of the daugh - ter of the Em - per-our of Ire-lande _____ and she sighed _____ af - ter her-self _____ as were _____ she born to bride with Tris - tis _____ Tris - ti - or _____ Tris -

Oct. 17, 1947

To Francis Poulenc and Pierre Bernac

Mélodies passagères

1. Puisque tout passe

original key: a minor third lower

Rainer Maria Rilke
Poèmes français

Samuel Barber
Op. 27, No. 1
1950

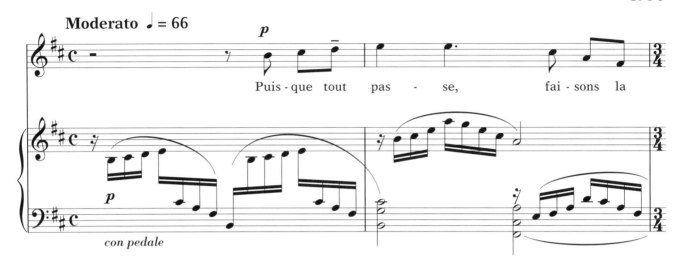

Puis-que tout pas - se, fai-sons la

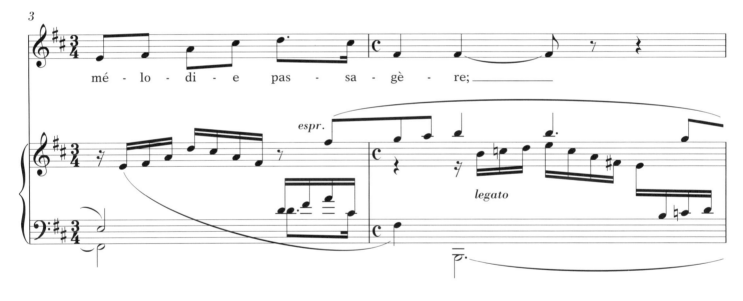

mé - lo - di - e pas - sa - gè - re;

cel - le qui nous dés - al -

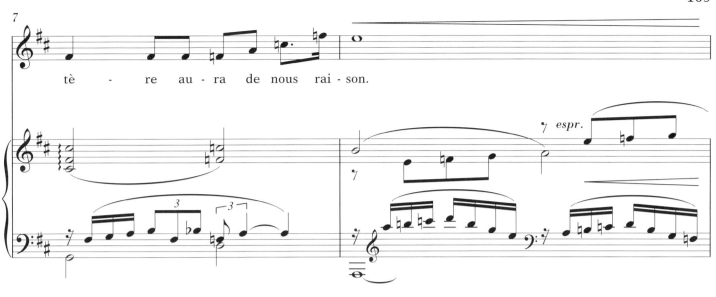

tè - re au - ra de nous rai - son.

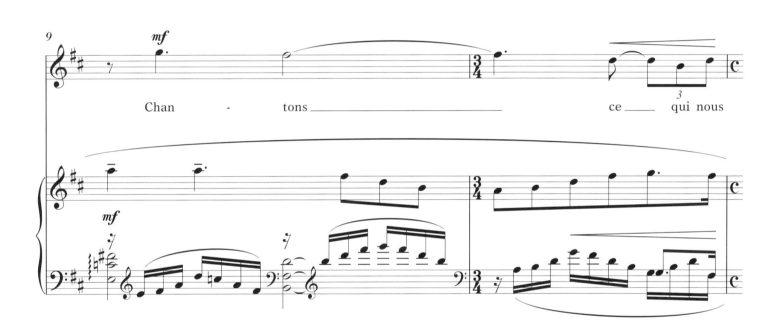

Chan - tons _____ ce ____ qui nous

quit - te a - vec a - mour et

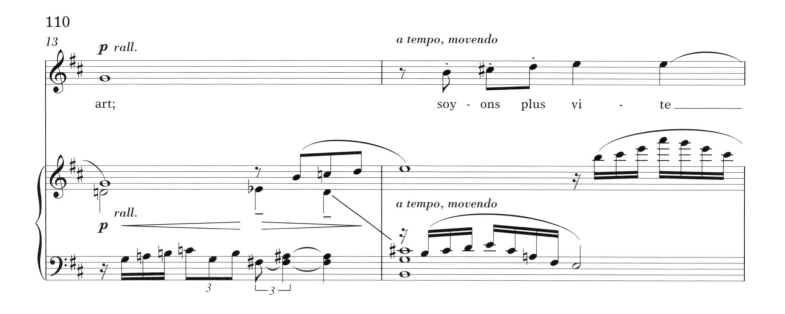

Jan. 1950

2. Un cygne

original key: a minor third lower

Rainer Maria Rilke
Poèmes français

Samuel Barber
Op. 27, No. 2
1951

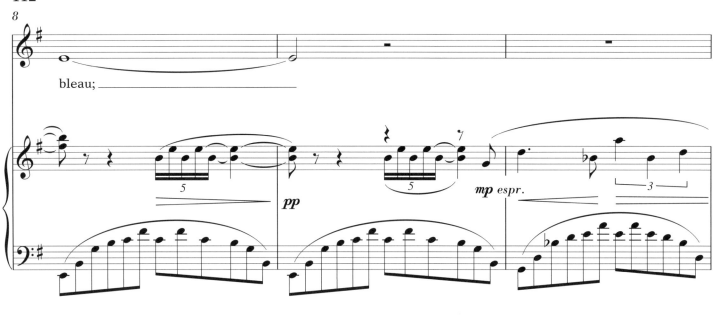

bleau;

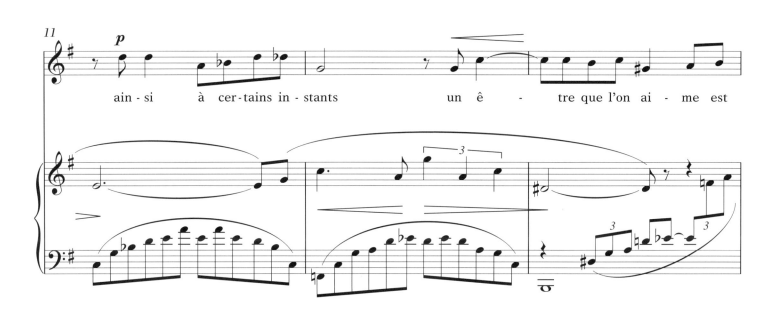

ain - si   à cer - tains in - stants   un ê -   tre que l'on ai - me est

tout un es - pa - ce mou - vant.

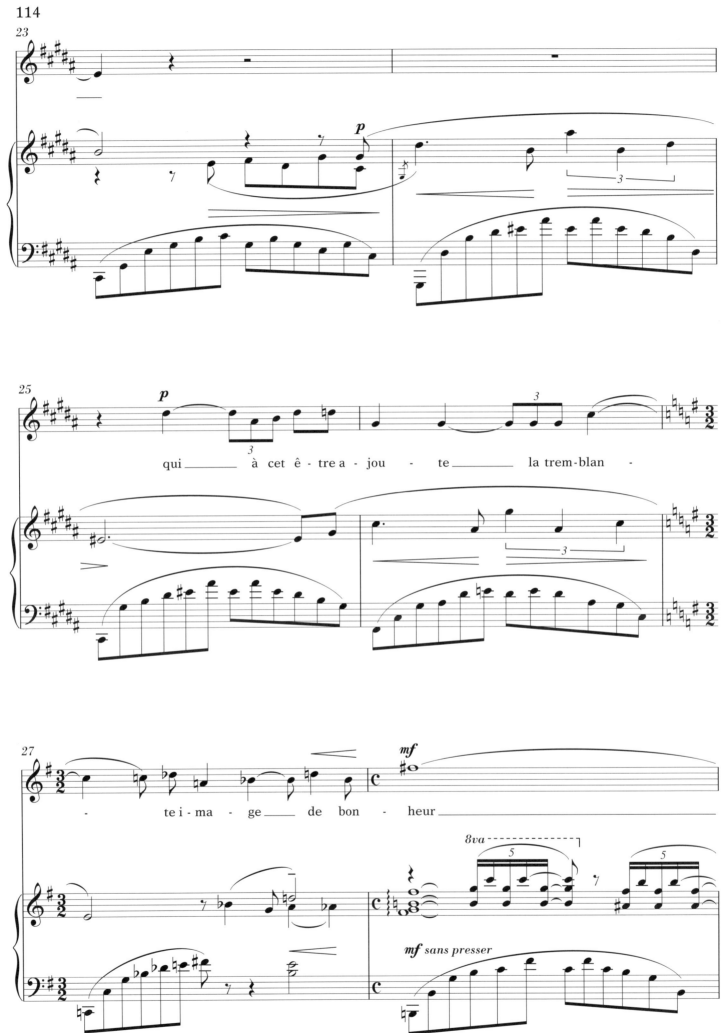

qui ____ à cet ê - tre a - jou - te ____ la trem-blan -

- te i - ma - ge ____ de bon - heur ____

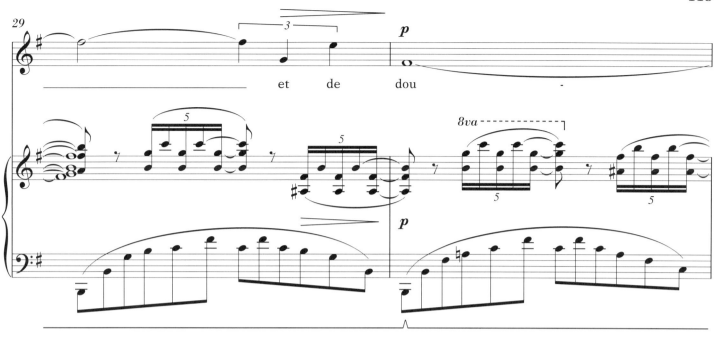

et de dou -

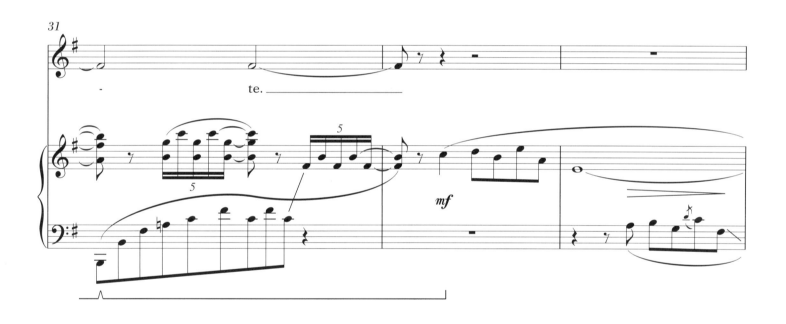

- te.

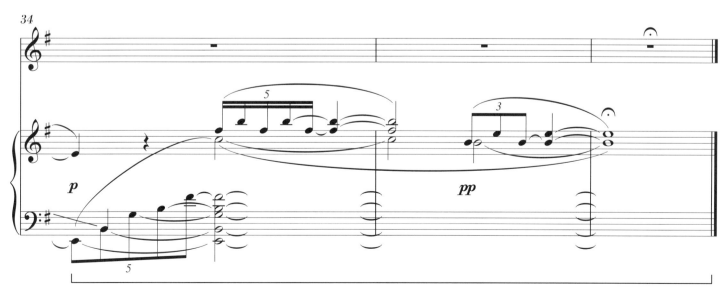

April 21, 1951

3. Tombeau dans un parc

original key: a minor third lower

Rainer Maria Rilke
Poèmes français

Samuel Barber
Op. 27, No. 3
1951

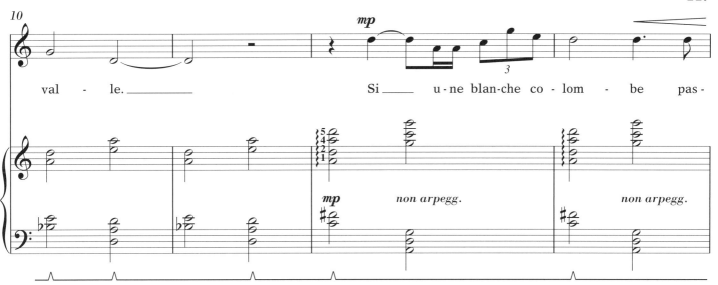

val - le. _____ Si _____ u - ne blan-che co - lom - be pas -

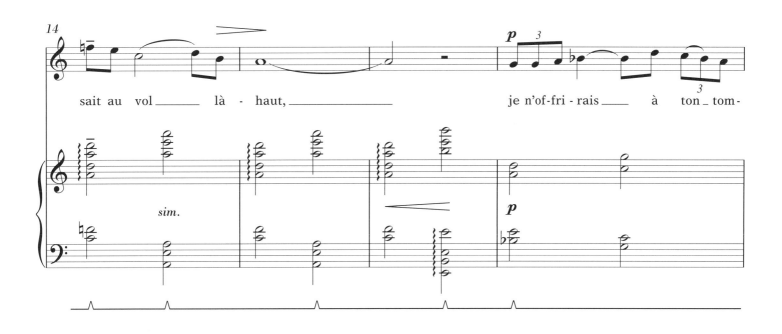

sait au vol _____ là - haut, _____ je n'of-fri - rais _____ à ton _ tom-

beau que son om - bre qui tom - be.

April 26, 1951

4. Le clocher chante

original key: a major second lower

Rainer Maria Rilke
Poèmes français

Samuel Barber
Op. 27, No. 4
1950

Cha-que di-man-che, ton par ton, ___ je leur jet-te ma man - ne; ___

qu'il soit bon, mon ca-ril-lon, ___ aux Va-lai-san - nes.

Feb. 16, 1950

5. Départ

original key: a major second lower

Rainer Maria Rilke
Poèmes français

Samuel Barber
Op. 27, No. 5
1950

Mon a - mi - e, il faut que je

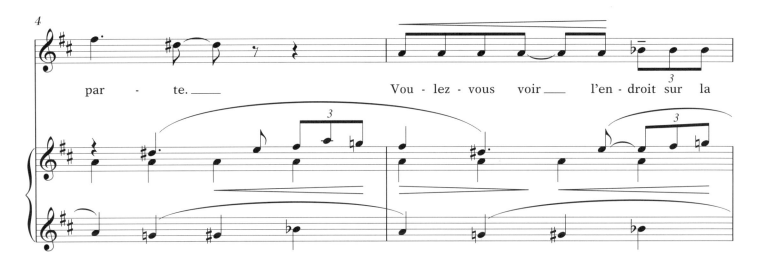

par - te. Vou - lez - vous voir l'en - droit sur la

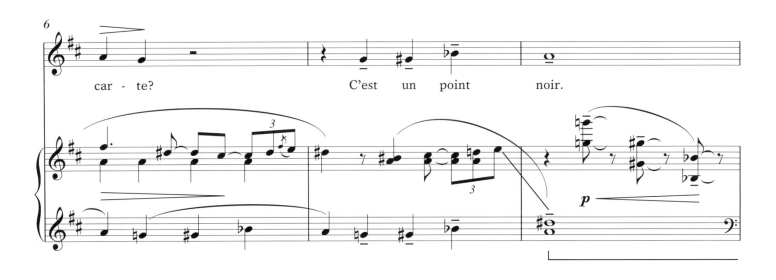

car - te? C'est un point noir.

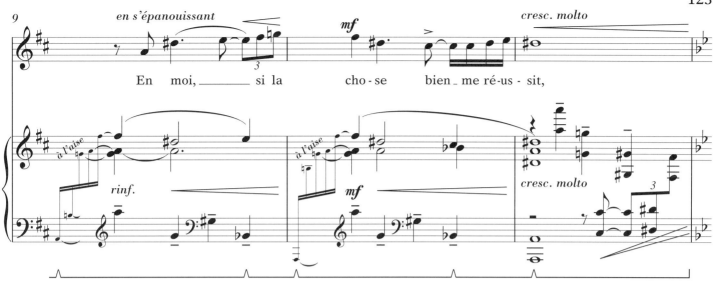

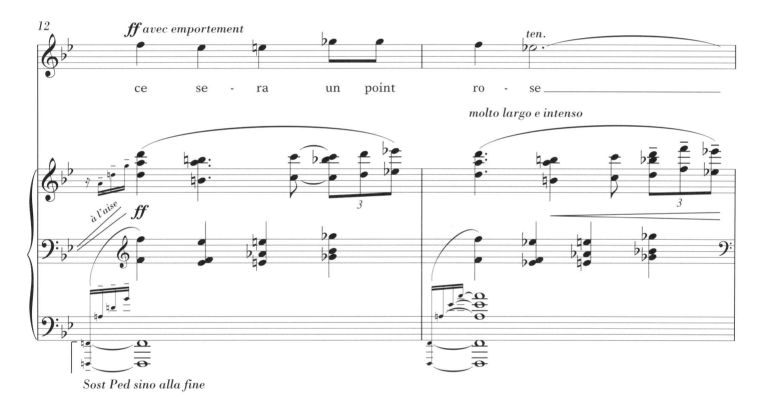

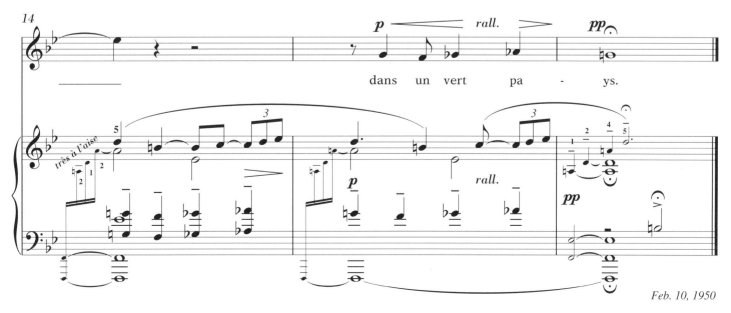

Feb. 10, 1950

Hermit Songs

To Elizabeth Sprague Coolidge

I. At Saint Patrick's Purgatory

original key

13th century
Translated by Sean O'Faolain

Samuel Barber
Op. 29, No. 1
1952

Text from *The Silver Branch* by Sean O'Faolain, copyright 1938 by The Viking Press, Inc., by permission of The Viking Press, Inc., New York, and Jonathan Cape Limited, London.

*Loch Derg (Red Lake) in County Donegal has been a place of pilgrimage from very early times.

by whom all men were made, who shunned not the death by three ___ wounds, ___

pi-ty me ___ on my pil-grim-age to Loch Derg ___

and I ___ with a

heart ___ not sof - ter than a stone! ___

Nov. 17, 1952

II. Church Bell at Night
original key

12th century
Translated by Howard Mumford Jones

Samuel Barber
Op. 29, No. 2
1952

Sweet lit-tle bell, struck on a wind-y night,
I would lie-fer keep tryst with thee Than be
With a light and fool-ish wo-man.

Text from *Romanesque Lyric,* by permission of the University of North Carolina Press.

Nov. 3, 1952

III. St. Ita's* Vision
original key

Attributed to Saint Ita, 8th century
Translated by Chester Kallman

Samuel Barber
Op. 29, No. 3
1953

"I will take noth-ing from my Lord," said she, "un-less He gives me His Son from

Heav-en   In the form of a Ba-by that I may   nurse Him." _ So that

Christ came down to her   in the form of a   Ba - by __ and then she   said:

*Ita – pronounce Eeta
Words used by special permission.

Ma - ry the Jew-ess by Heav - en's Light. In - fant Je - sus,

at my breast, what King is there but You who could

Give ev-er-last - ing Good? where for I give my food.

Jan. 9, 1953

IV. The Heavenly Banquet

original key

Attributed to Saint Brigid, 10th century
Translated by Sean O'Faolain

Samuel Barber
Op. 29, No. 4
1952

Lively, with good humor ♩ = 108

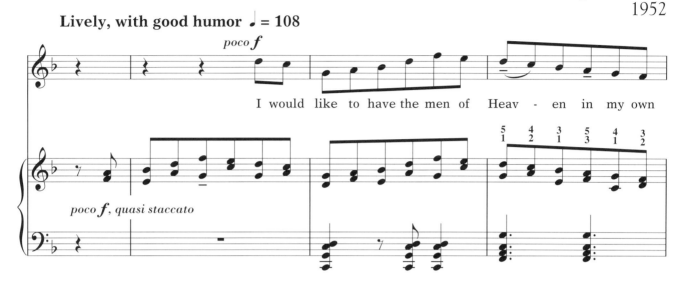

I would like to have the men of Heav - en in my own

house; with vats of good cheer laid out for them. I would like to have the three

Mar - ys, their fame is so great. I would like peo - ple from ev - 'ry

Text from *The Silver Branch* by Sean O'Faolain, copyright 1938, by the Viking Press, Inc., by permission of The Viking Press, Inc., New York, and Jonathan Cape Limited, London.

cor-ner of Heav-en.

I would like them to be cheer-ful in their drink-ing:

I would like— to have Je - sus sit-ting here a-

mong— them.

I would like a great lake of beer—— for the

King of Kings.

I would like to be watch-ing Heav - en's fam - i - ly

Drink ing it through all e - ter - ni - ty.

Nov. 13, 1952

V. The Crucifixion

original key

From The Speckled Book, 12th Century
Translated by Howard Mumford Jones

Samuel Barber
Op. 29, No. 5
1952

Text from *Romanesque Lyric,* by permission of the University of North Carolina Press.

Ah, _____ sore was the suff-'ring borne By the bod-y of Ma-ry's

Son, _____ But sor-er still to Him was the grief Which for His sake _____

Tempo I

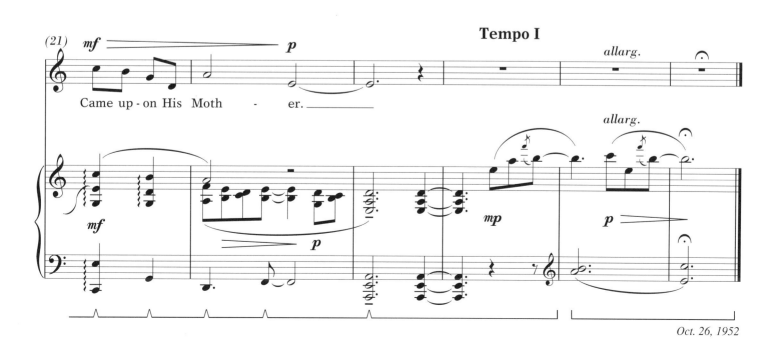

Came up-on His Moth - er. _____

Oct. 26, 1952

VI. Sea-Snatch
original key

8th–9th century
Translated by Kenneth Jackson

Samuel Barber
Op. 29, No. 6
1953

Text from Kenneth Jackson's *A Celtic Miscellany,* by permission of Routledge and Kegan Paul, Ltd., London, and Harvard University Press, Cambridge, Mass.

sumed us, swal-lowed us, as tim-ber is de - voured_ by crim-son fire _ from Heav-en.

It has bro-ken us, it has crushed us, it has drowned _ us, O _

King _ of the star-bright King-dom of Heav-en!

Jan. 6, 1953

VII. Promiscuity
original key

9th century
Translated by Kenneth Jackson

Samuel Barber
Op. 29, No. 7
1953

Jan. 15, 1953

Text from Kenneth Jackson's *A Celtic Miscellany,* by permission of Routledge and Kegan Paul, Ltd., London, and Harvard University Press, Cambridge, Mass.

*Edan: pronounce Ay-den.

To Isabelle Vengerova

VIII. The Monk and His Cat
original key

8th or 9th century
Translated by W.H. Auden

Samuel Barber
Op. 29, No. 8
1953

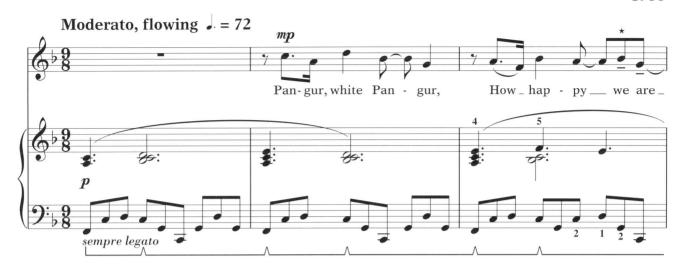

Pan-gur, white Pan - gur, How _ hap - py _ we are _

A - lone to - geth-er, _ Scho - lar and cat. _

Each _ has his _ own _ work to do dai - ly; _

senza ped.

Words used by special permission.
*Notes marked (–) in these two measures should be slightly longer, pochissimo rubato; also on the fourth page. [Barber's footnote]

For you it is hunt-ing, for me stud-y.

Your shin - ing eye

watch - es the wall; my fee - ble eye is fixed on a

book.

You re-joice when your claws En-trap a mouse;

Feb. 16, 1953

To the memory of Mary Evans Scott

IX. The Praises of God
original key

11th century
Translated by W.H. Auden

Samuel Barber
Op. 29, No. 9
1953

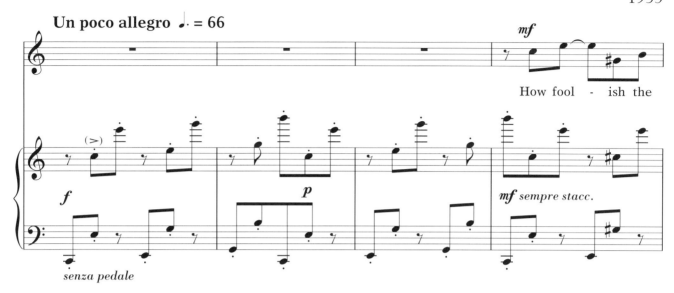

Words used by special permission.

To Whom __ the light birds With no soul but

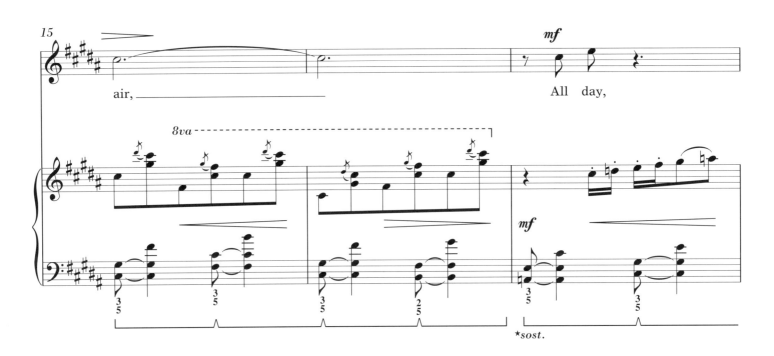

air, _____ All day,

ev - 'ry-where all day, ev - 'ry-where,

*Pedal markings in measures 17–20 are for the sostenuto pedal.

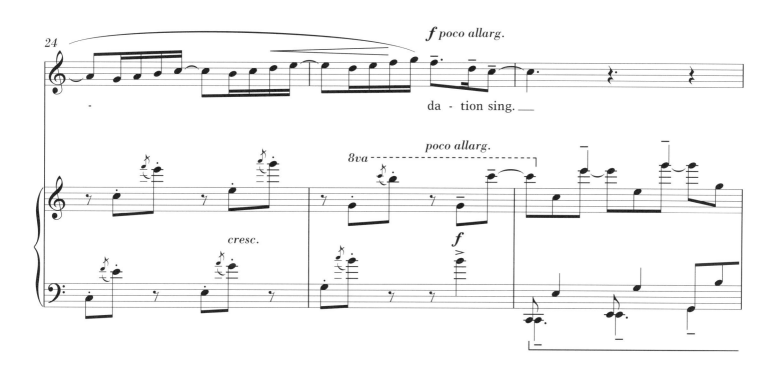

Jan. 27, 1953

X. The Desire for Hermitage
original key

8th–9th century
Based on a translation by Sean O'Faolain

Samuel Barber
Op. 29, No. 10
1953

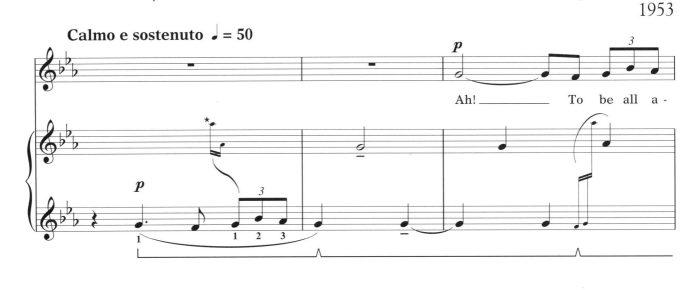

Text from *The Silver Branch* by Sean O'Faolain, copyright 1938 by The Viking Press, Inc., by permission of The Viking Press, Inc., New York, and Jonathan Cape Limited, London.
*All grace-notes somewhat longer, rubato. [Barber's footnote]

To my friend Leontyne Price

Despite and Still
1. A Last Song*

original key

Robert Graves

Samuel Barber
Op. 41, No. 1
1968

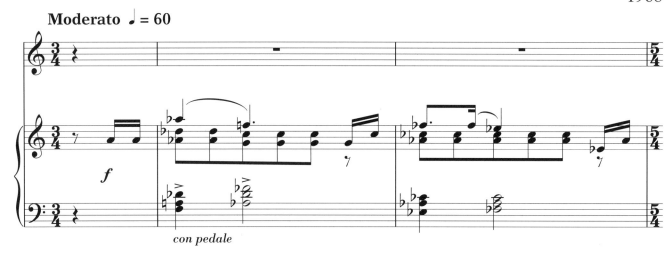

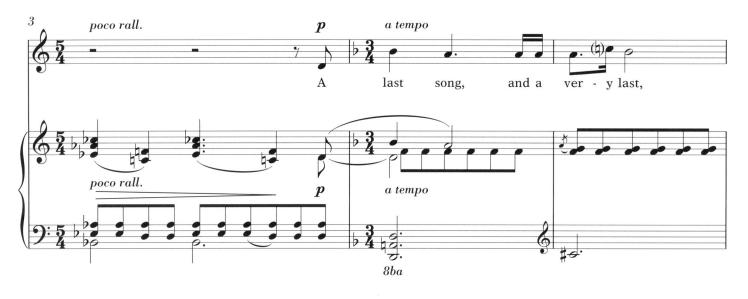

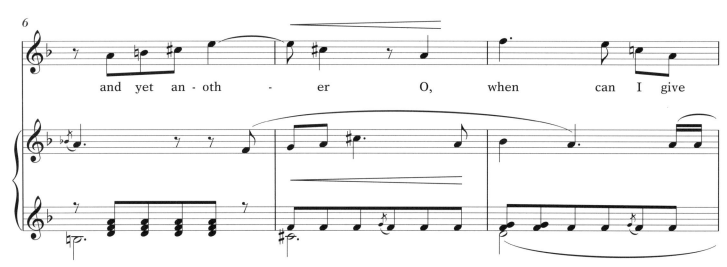

*In the original: "A Last Poem."
Poem used by permission.

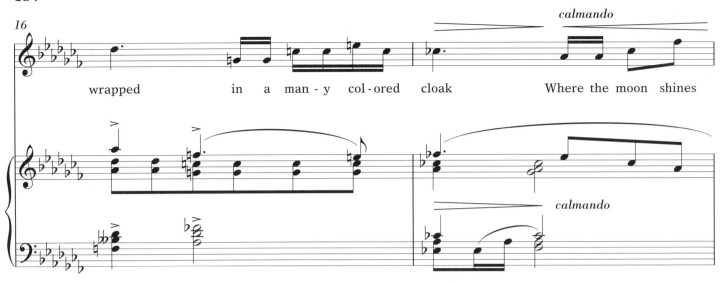

wrapped in a man-y col-ored cloak Where the moon shines

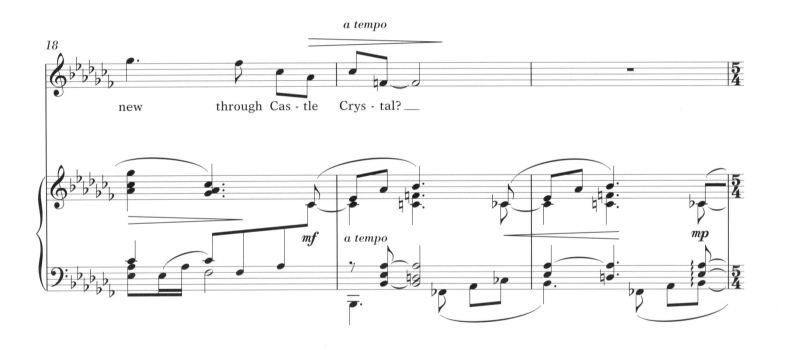

new through Cas-tle Crys-tal?

Tempo I

Shall I nev-er hear her whis-per soft-ly:

"But this is truth _____ writ - ten by you on - ly _____

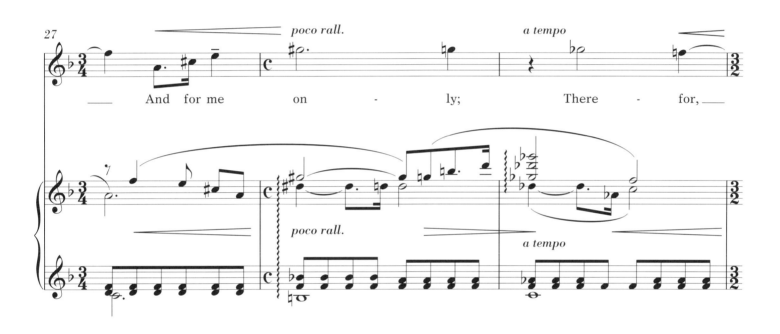

poco rall.   a tempo

_____ And for me on - ly; There - for, _____

poco rall.   a tempo

allargando e morendo

_____ love, _____ have done?" _____

allargando e morendo

sf   p mf   p   pp

June, 1968
Santa Cristina

2. My Lizard
(Wish for a Young Love)
original key

Theodore Roethke

Samuel Barber
Op. 41, No. 2
1968

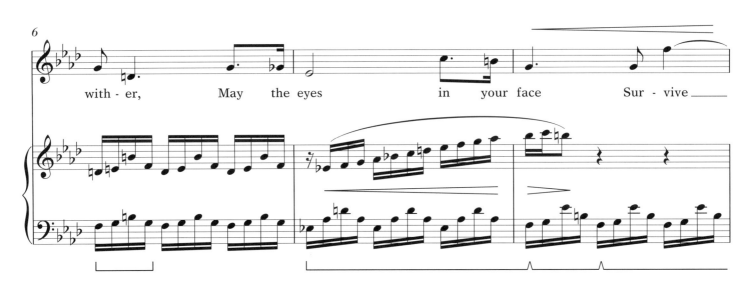

July 20, 1968
Santa Cristina

3. In the Wilderness
original key

Robert Graves

Samuel Barber
Op. 41, No. 3
1968

Slightly slower than tempo I

Then ev - er with him went,

Of all his wan - der-ings Com-rade, with _ rag - ged coat, Gaunt ribs, poor in - no-cent

Bleed-ing _ foot, burn-ing _ throat, _ The guile-less young scape -

goat:

For for - ty nights and days

Fol - lowed in Je - sus' ways, Sure guard be - hind him kept.

Tears ___ like a lov - er wept. ___

Aug. 3, 1968
Santa Cristina

4. Solitary Hotel

original key

James Joyce

Samuel Barber
Op. 41, No. 4
1968

Like a rather fast tango in 2 ♩ = 60

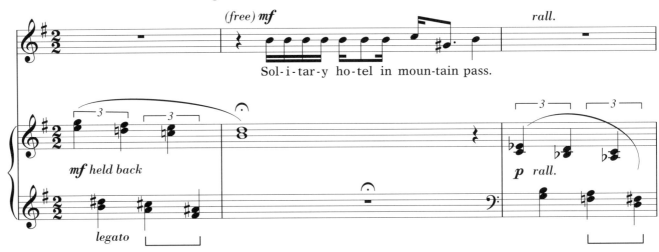

Sol-i-tar-y ho-tel in moun-tain pass.

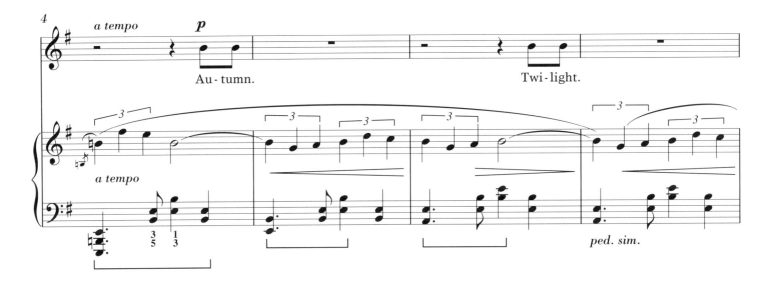

Au-tumn. Twi-light.

Fire lit. In dark cor-ner young___ man seat-ed.

Text reprinted by permission of The Society of Authors as the literary representative of the Estate of James Joyce.

5. Despite and Still

original key

Robert Graves

Samuel Barber
Op. 41, No. 5
1968

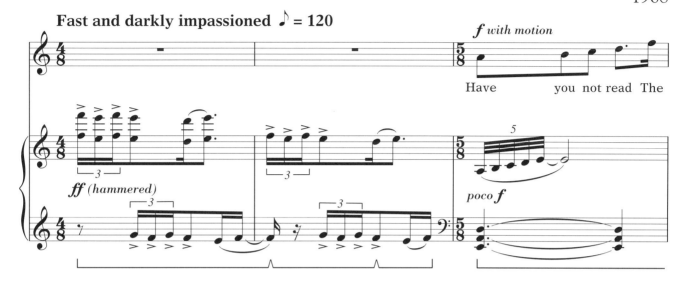

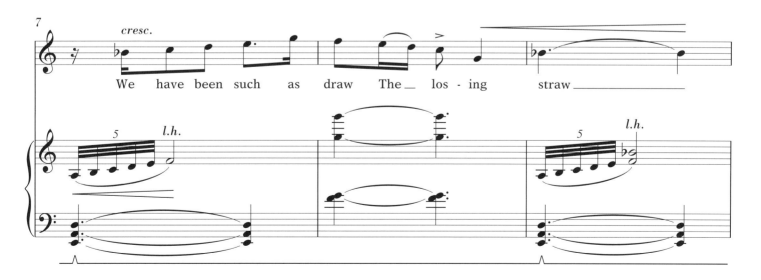

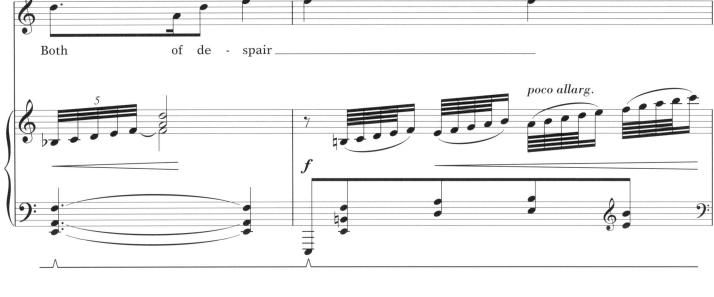

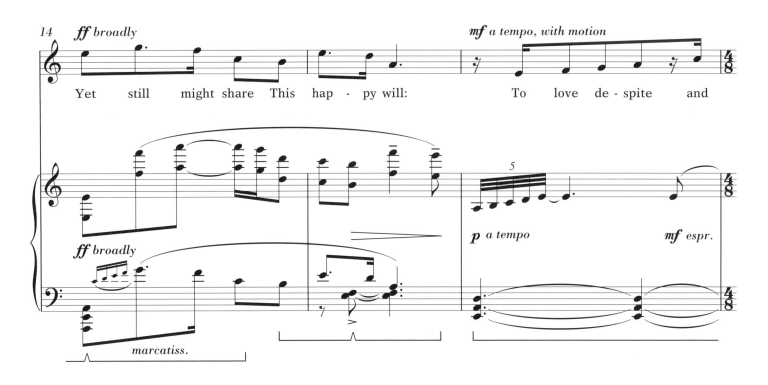

still, To love de - spite and still.

Nev - er let us de - ny

The thing's ne - ces - si - ty But, o, re - fuse

Aug. 14, 1968
Santa Cristina

Now have I fed and eaten up the rose

original key: A minor

James Joyce
(from the German of Gottfried Keller)

Samuel Barber
Op. 45, No. 1
1972

Reprinted by permission of The Society of Authors as the literary representative of the Estate of James Joyce.

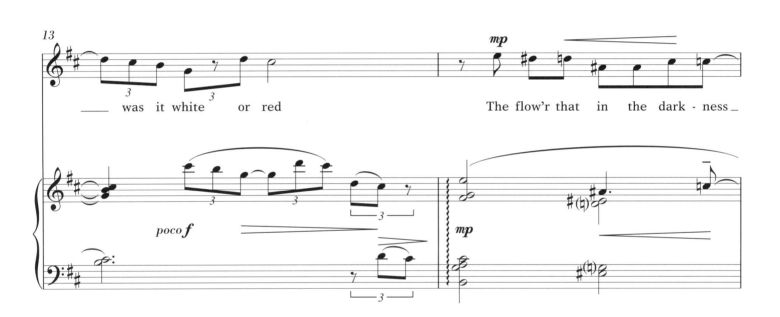

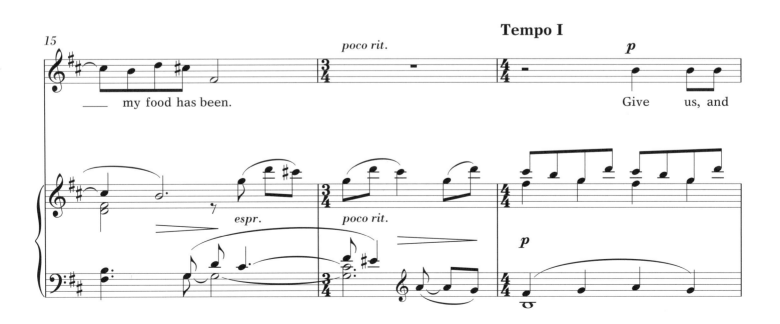

if Thou give,_____ thy dai - ly bread,   De - liv - er us from

e - vil, Lord,   A - men._____

Spoleto, March 1972

A Green Lowland of Pianos

original key: a major second lower

Czeslaw Milosz
(from the Polish of Jerzy Harasymowicz)

Samuel Barber
Op. 45, No. 2
1972

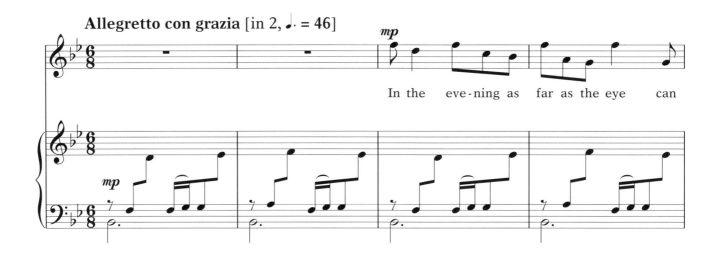

In the eve-ning as far as the eye can

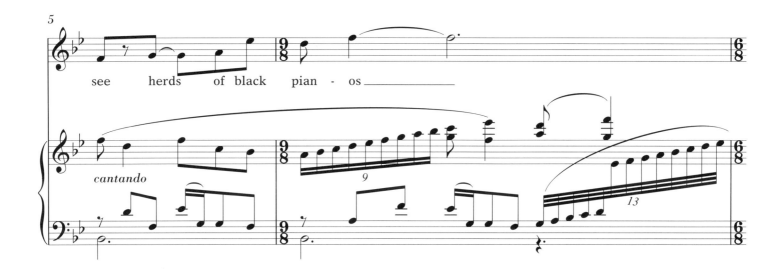

see herds of black pian - os

up to their knees in the mire _ they lis - ten to the frogs

they gur-gle in wa-ter with chords_ of rap - ture___

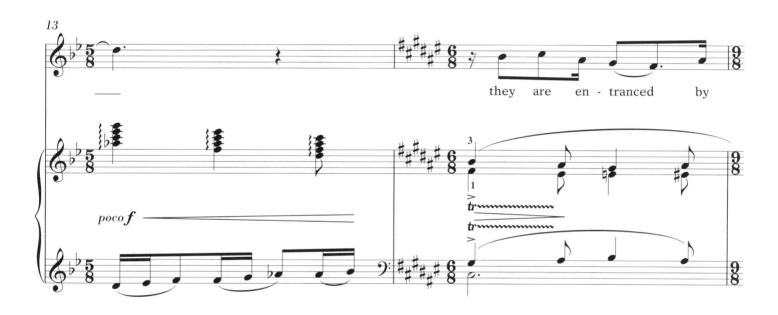

___ they are en - tranced by

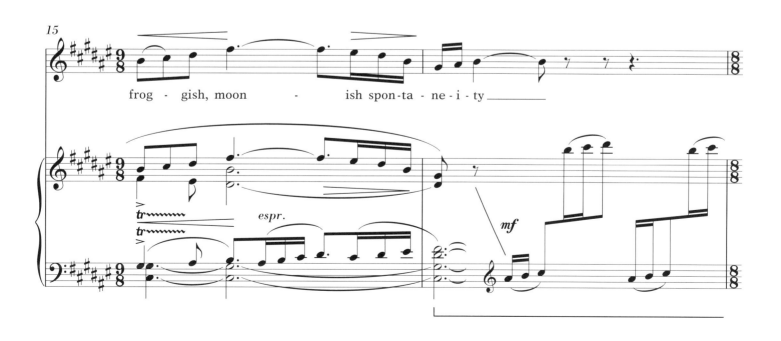

frog - gish, moon - ish spon-ta - ne - i - ty___

looking with in-dif-fer-ence ____ at the white flow - ers of ____ the aud - ience ____

at the ges-tic - u -lating of ____ the ush -

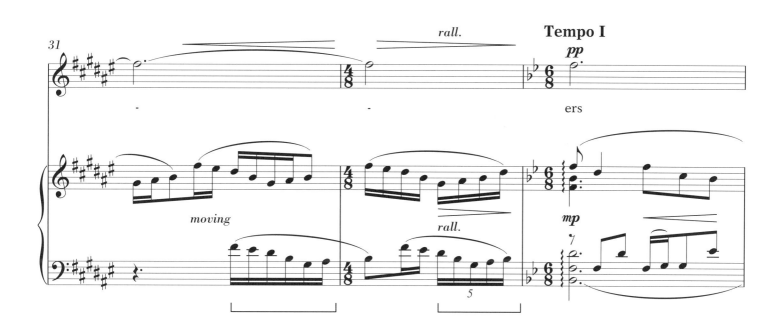

- - ers

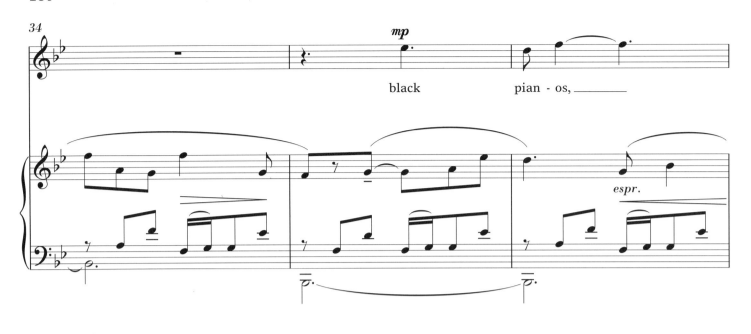

black pian - os, _____

black pian - os. _____

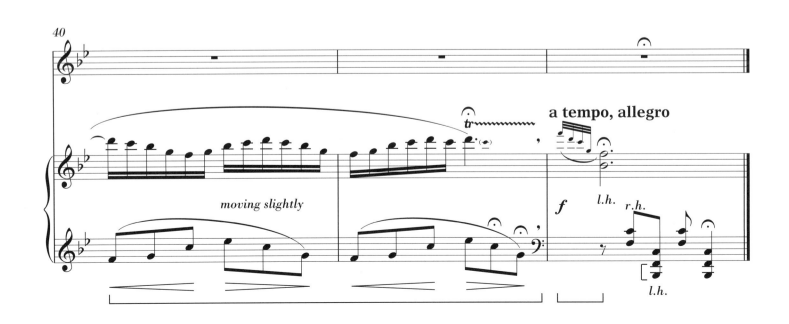

O boundless, boundless evening

original key: G Major

Christopher Middleton
(from the German of George Heym)

Samuel Barber
Op. 45, No. 3
1972

now, rich - hued by sun.

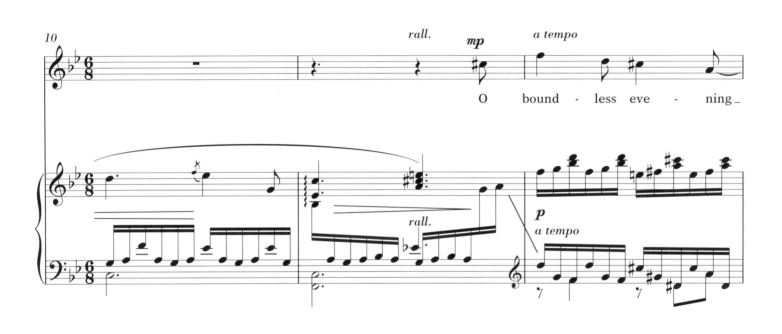

O bound - less eve - ning _

____ where the corn - fields throw The scat-tered day - light ____

back in an au - re - ole.

Swal - lows high up are sing - ing, ver - y

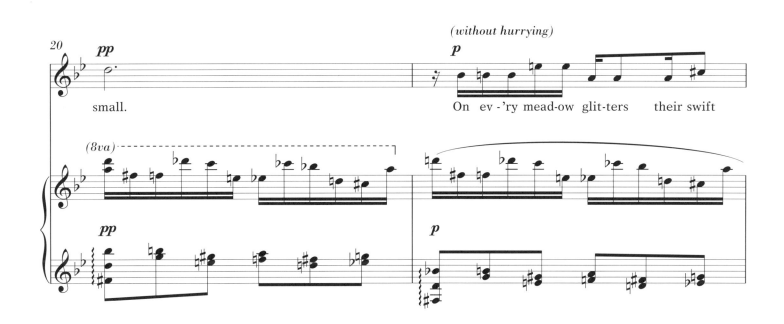

small. On ev -'ry mead-ow glit-ters their swift

flight,＿＿＿ In woods＿＿＿ of rush - es and where tall

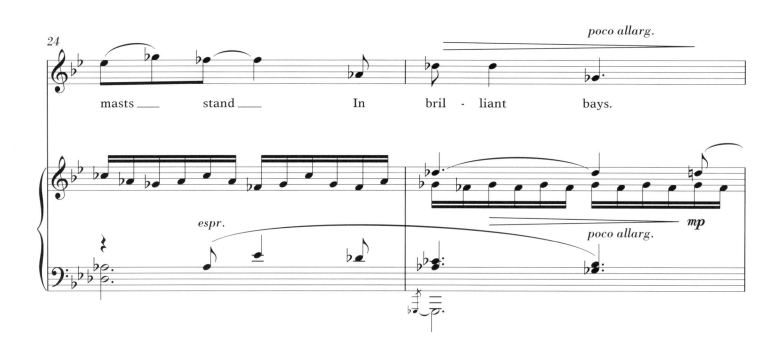

masts＿ stand＿ In bril - liant bays.

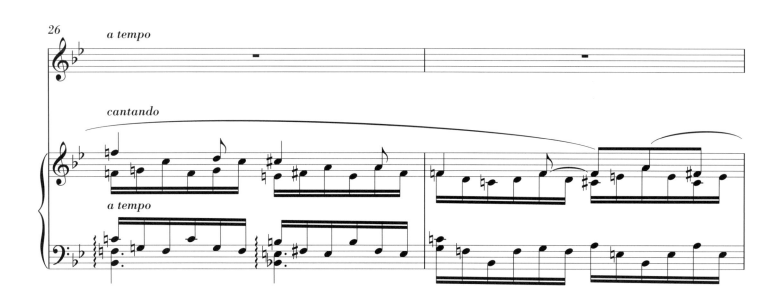

poco più sostenuto

Yet in ra- vines be-yond Be-tween the hills al-read - y nests the night.

August 17, 1972

SONGS PUBLISHED POSTHUMOUSLY

Barber indicated few dynamics in most of the manuscripts of posthumously published songs in this section. Minimal editorial suggestions appear in brackets throughout.

Ask me to rest

original key

Edward Hicks Streeter Terry

Samuel Barber
1926

hap - pi-ness: Then will I heed thy plea; But

now— with no - thing done— I could not rest; My

heart would break with pent-up a - gon-y. Ask me to

rest _____ when Hate and Greed are stilled, _____ When War-fare's

Au clair de la lune

original key: a major second lower

Anonymous (18th century)

Samuel Barber
1926

Mournfully, con moto

[*p*]

Au clair de la lu - ne,

Mon a - mi Pier - rot,

Prê - te - moi ta plu - me

Fantasy in Purple

original key: a major second lower

Langston Hughes

Samuel Barber
1925

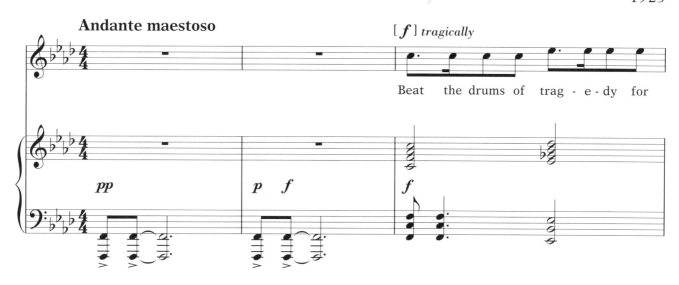

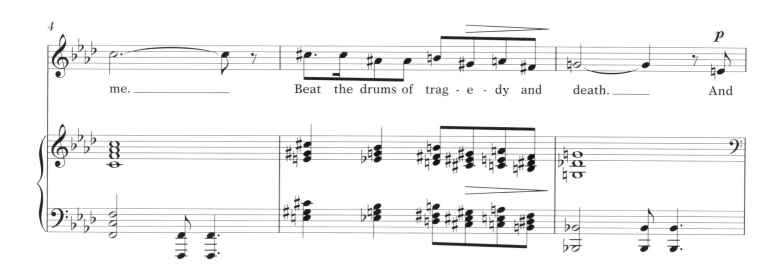

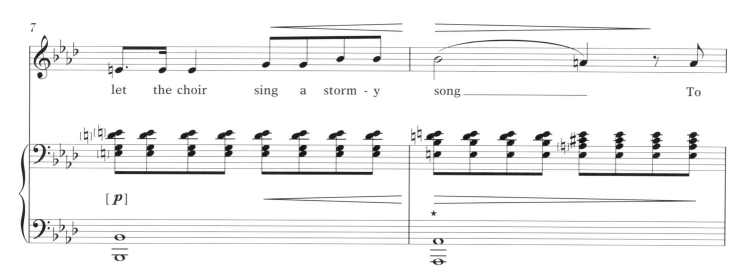

*Barber may have intended A-naturals in the bass clef, though no accidentals appear in the manuscript.

*The manuscript indicates an A as the lowest note of the left hand; the pattern would suggest a G.

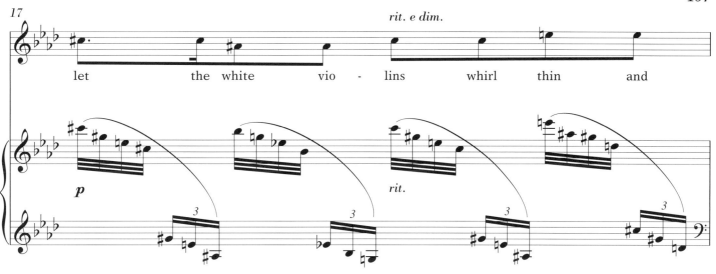

let the white vio - lins whirl thin and

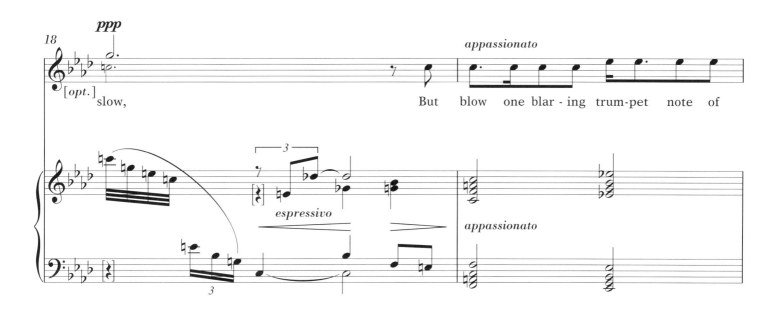

slow, But blow one blar - ing trum-pet note of

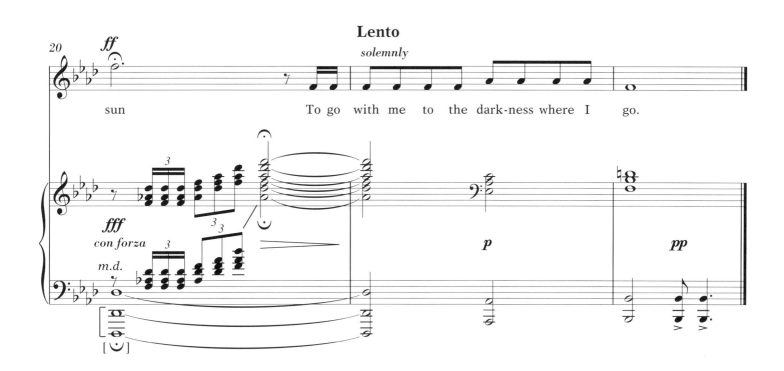

sun To go with me to the dark-ness where I go.

Beggar's Song

original key: E-flat Major

William Henry Davies

Samuel Barber
1936

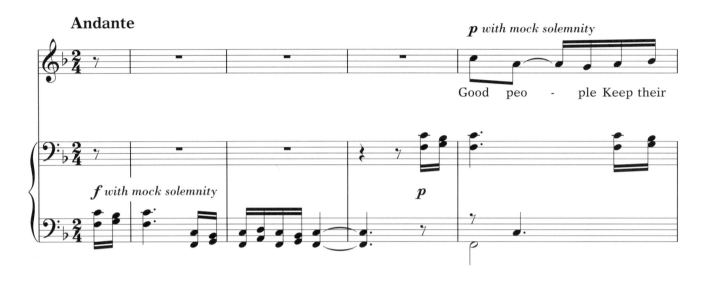

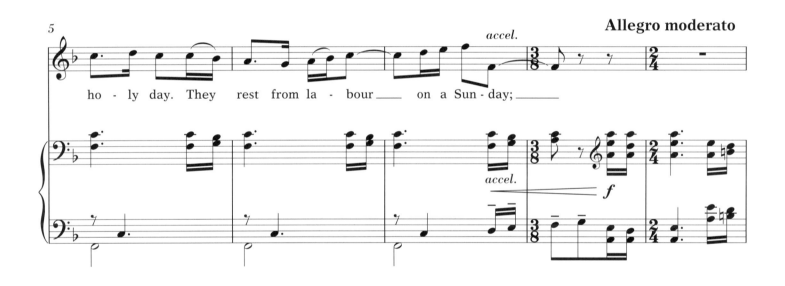

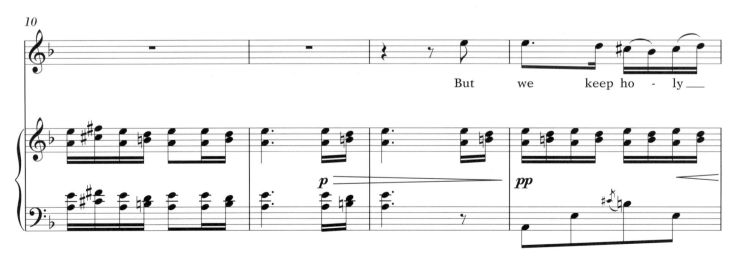

Text used by permission.

In the dark pinewood

original key: a major second lower

James Joyce

Samuel Barber
1937

Text used by permission.

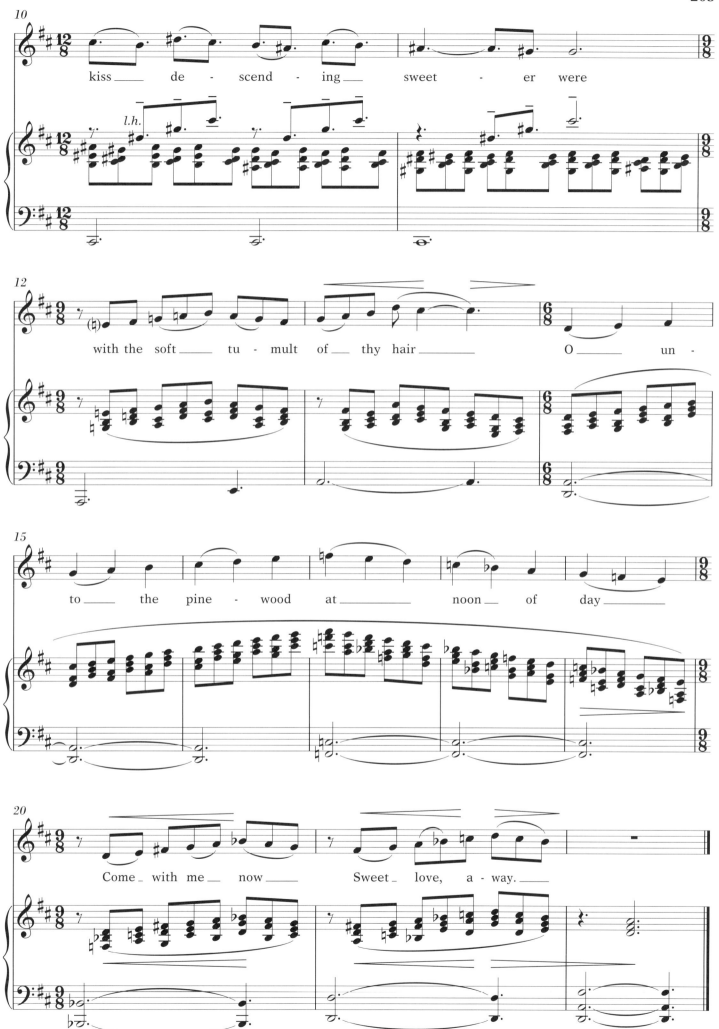

La nuit

original key

Alfred Meurath

Samuel Barber
1925

Sostenuto

La nuit c'est _ l'heure du songe Des

rêves, _____ et de l'a - mour, De la dou - leur qui nous

ronge, Et la fin des maux de ce jour. _____

sol - i-tude et l'enn - ui; Trou-bles en no - tre con-science, Car _ elle _

songe _ la _ nuit. _ Et

Tempo primo

songe à de tris - tes choses, Car là dans l'ombre est l'a - bîme! _ Heu -

reux _ l'homme qui re - pose, Et dort dans la nuit su - blime!

Love at the Door

original key: G-sharp minor

from the Greek *Meleager*
Translated by John Addington Symonds

Samuel Barber
1934

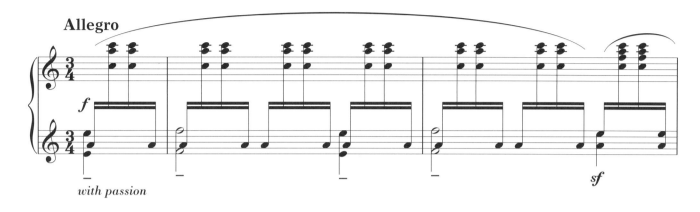

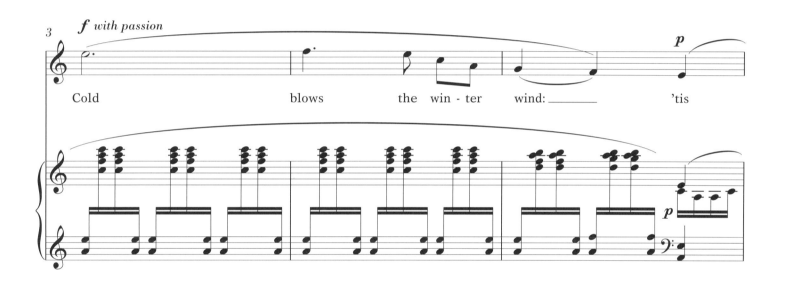

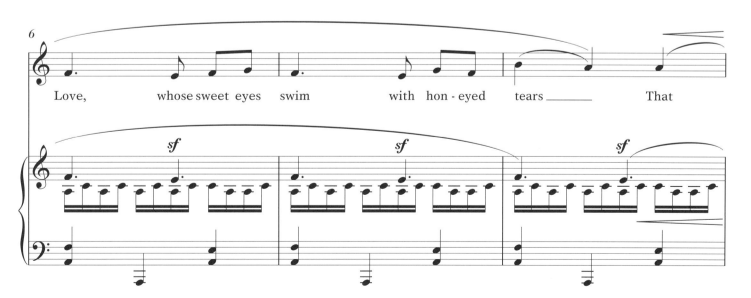

Text used by permission.

Meno mosso

for my wan-d'ring sail A - drift up - on these waves of love Safe har - bor from the whis - tling gale.

Love's Caution

original key: a diminished third lower

William Henry Davies

Samuel Barber
1935

[Moderato]

Tell them, when you are home a-gain, How warm the air was now;

How si - lent were the birds and leaves, And of the moon's full glow;

And how we saw a - far a fall ing star. It was a tear of pure de - light

Text used by permission.

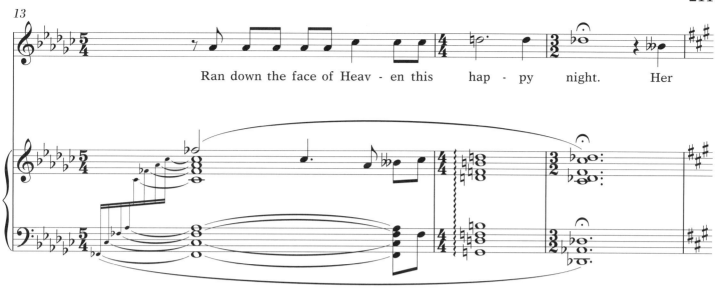

Ran down the face of Heav - en this hap - py night. Her

Poco a poco più mosso

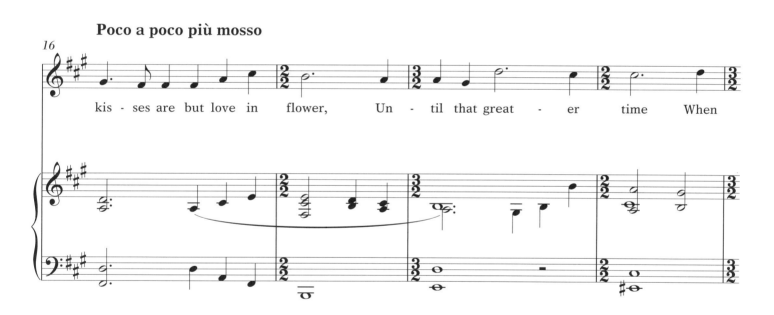

kis - ses are but love in flower, Un - til that great - er time When

gath -'ring strength, those flowers take wing, _____ And Love can

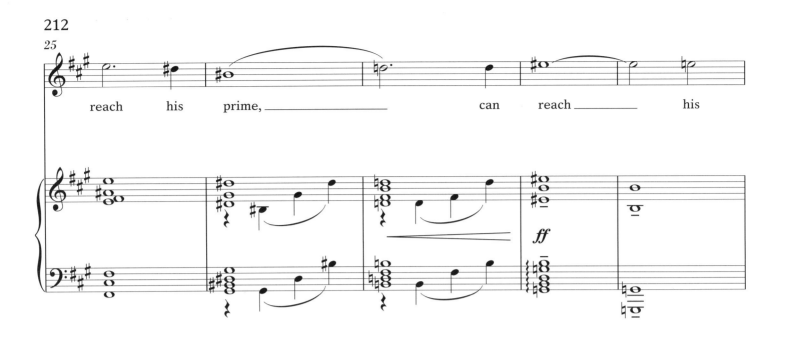

reach his prime, _____ can reach _____ his

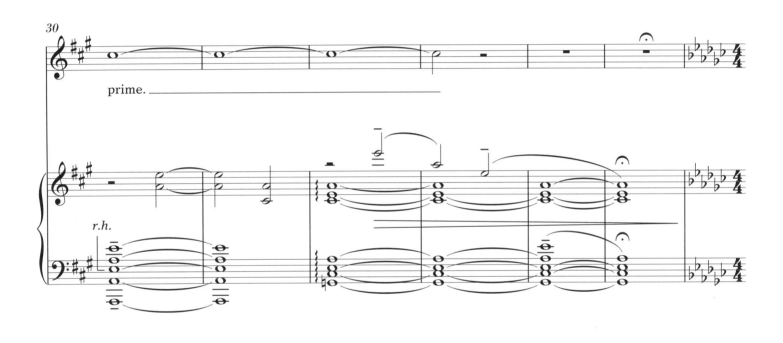

prime. _____

Tempo I

And now, and now, my heart's de-light, Good-night, good -

night; Give me, give me the last sweet

kiss, But do not breathe at home one

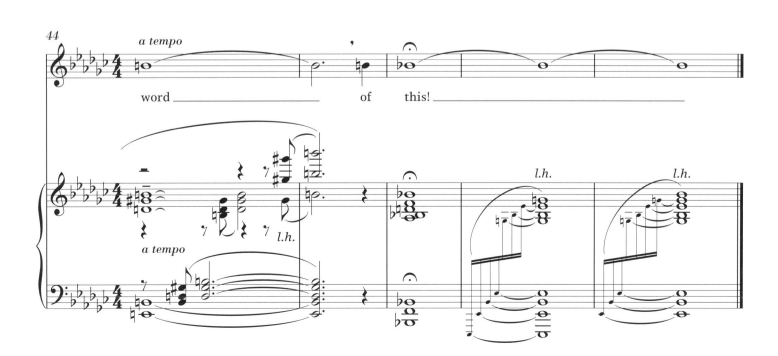

word _____ of this! _____

Man
original key

Humbert Wolfe

Samuel Barber
1926

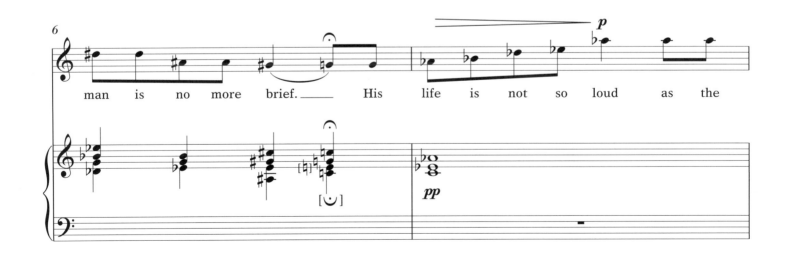

passing of a cloud; his death is qui-et-er than hare-bells, when they stir. The

years that have no form and sub-stance are as warm, and

space has hard-ly less su-preme an emp-ti-ness.

And

*Barber wrote only the right-hand notes on the first beat of measure 20. We assume he meant this figure to continue into measure 21.

*The manuscript clearly indicates an F-natural as the bottom note of the left-hand chord. This differs from measure 3.

Mother, I cannot mind my wheel

original key

Walter Savage Landor

Samuel Barber
1927

Of that so sweet imprisonment

original key: a minor third lower

James Joyce

Samuel Barber
1935

Of that so sweet im-pris-on-ment My soul,

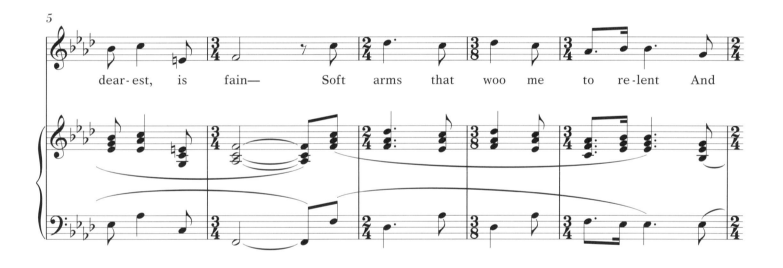

dear-est, is fain— Soft arms that woo me to re-lent And

woo me to de-tain._____ Ah,_____ could they ev-er

Text used by permission.

wise may __ trou - ble us; But sleep to __ dream - ier

sleep be __ wed, But sleep to __ dream - ier

sleep be ___ wed Where soul with soul lies

pris - on - ed. _____

Music, when soft voices die

original key

Percy Bysshe Shelley

Samuel Barber
c. 1925–1926

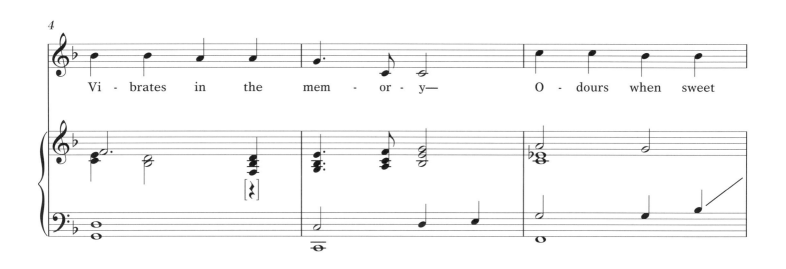

Rose leaves, when the rose is dead, Are heap'd for the be -

lov - ed's bed; And so thy thoughts when thou are gone,

Love it - self shall slumb - er on.

Night Wanderers

original key: a major second lower

William Henry Davies

Samuel Barber
1935

Text used by permission.

on hard, _____ cold wood _____ or stone,

I - ron, and ache in eve - ry bone;

They hate _____

___ the night, they see no eyes Of loved ____ ones in _____ the

Peace

original key: a minor third lower

Paul Elmer More
from the Sanskrit of Bhartrihari

Samuel Barber
1935

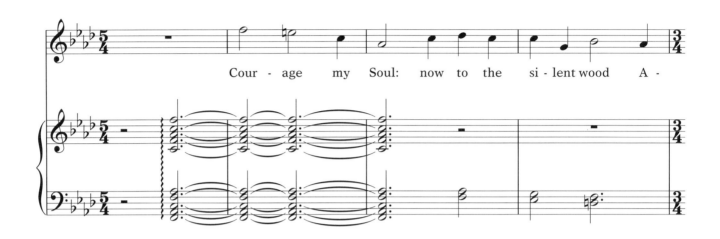

Barber's manuscript has no tempo marking. Except for mm. 15–16 he indicated no dynamics.

★The manuscript has an extra beat in the r.h. piano in m. 10, certainly a mistake. We have corrected it to what we believe was Barber's intention.

13
p
deep.
Thus loud au -
pp
17
thor - i - ty in fol - ly bold
And tongues that stam - mer with de -
21
sire for gold
And mur - mur★ of the wind - y world shall
25
cease Nor ech - o through our peace.

★The poem has "murmuring" here. Barber set "murmur," possibly his error.

Jan. 5, '35

Serenader
original key: a major second lower

George H. Dillon

Samuel Barber
1934

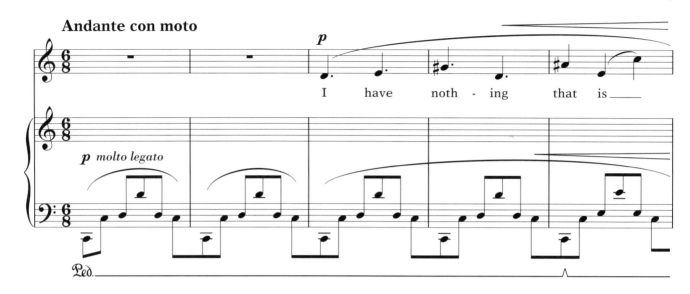

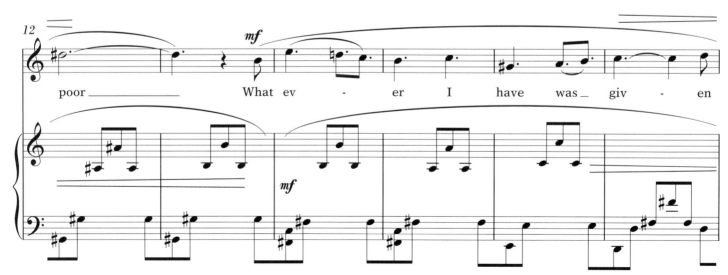

Text used by permission.

me: The earth, ___ the air, ___ the sun, ___ the sea ___

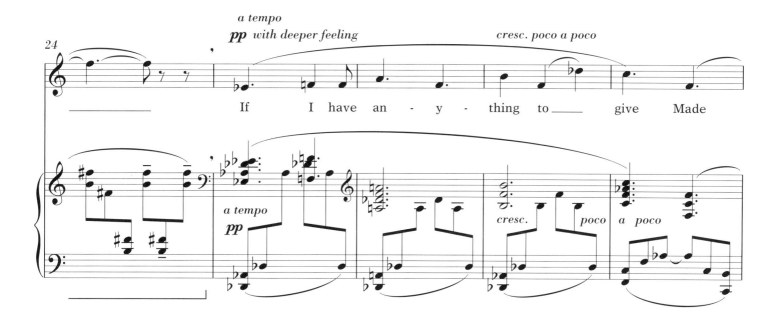

If I have an - y - thing to ___ give Made

sure - ly of the life ___ I live It ___ is a song that

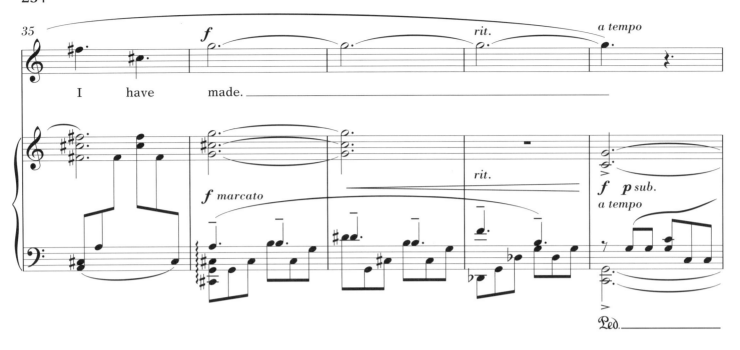

Un poco più lento

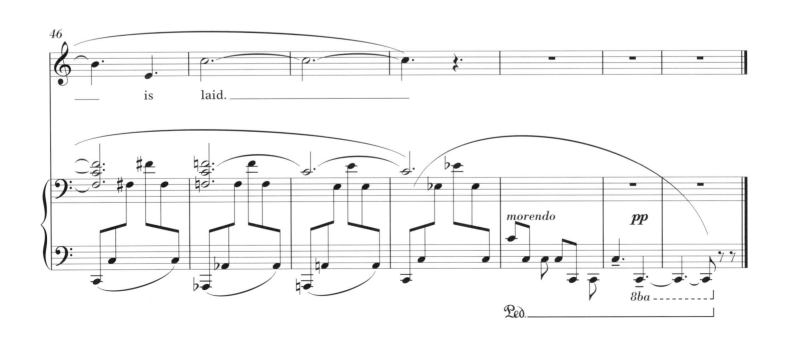

A Slumber Song of the Madonna

original key

Alfred Noyes

Samuel Barber
1925

Text used by permission.

Here in my arms as I sing thee to sleep! Hush - a - by

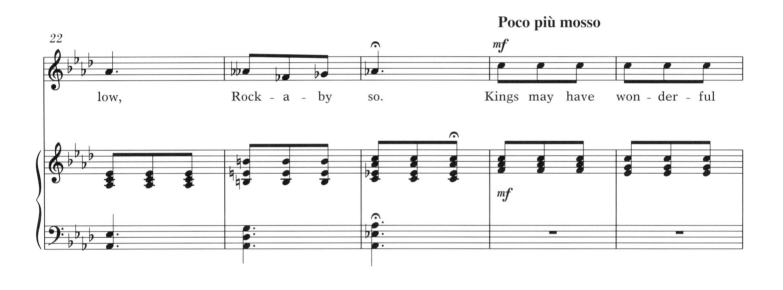

Poco più mosso

low, Rock - a - by so. Kings may have won - der - ful

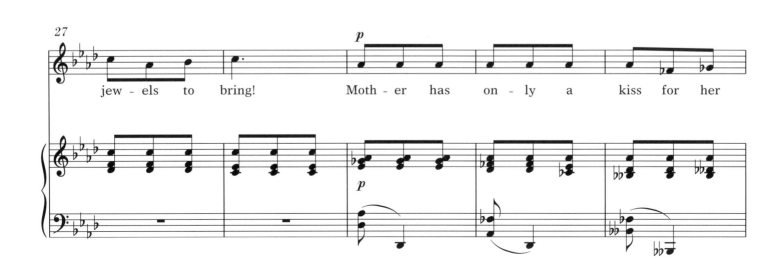

jew - els to bring! Moth - er has on - ly a kiss for her

king. Why should my sing - ing So make me to weep?

On - ly I know that I love thee, I love thee!

Tempo primo

Love thee, my lit-tle one, _____ Sleep!

Strings in the earth and air

original key

James Joyce

Samuel Barber
1935

Text used by permission.
Barber's manuscript indicates no tempo and few dynamics.

All soft - ly play - ing,   With

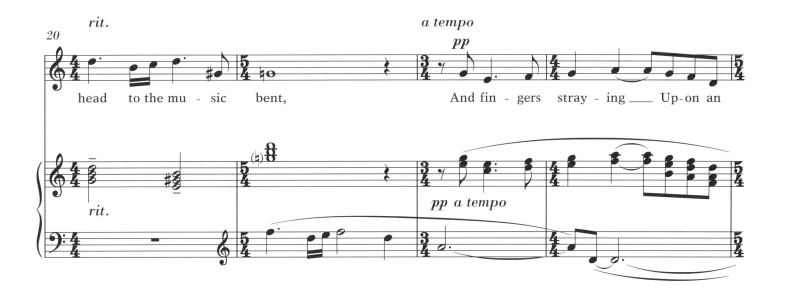

rit.   *a tempo*

head   to the mu - sic   bent,   And fin - gers stray - ing ___ Up-on an

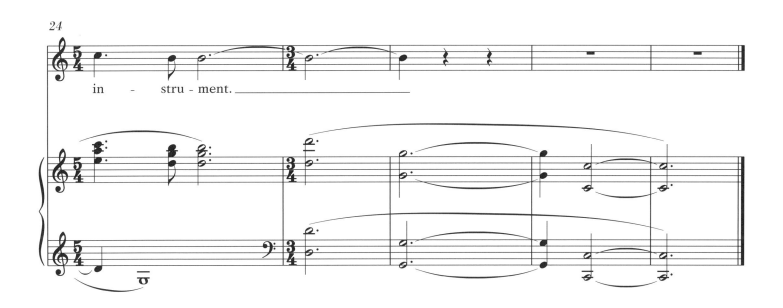

in - stru - ment. _____

There's nae lark

original key: E-flat Major

Algernon Charles Swinburne

Samuel Barber
1927

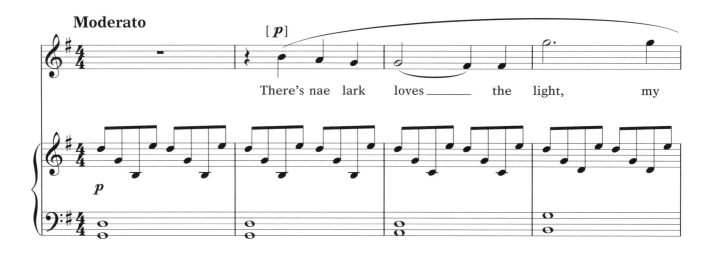

Text used by permission.

Stopping by Woods on a Snowy Evening

original key: E Major

Robert Frost

Samuel Barber
c. 1935–1936

Whose woods these are I think I know. His house is in the

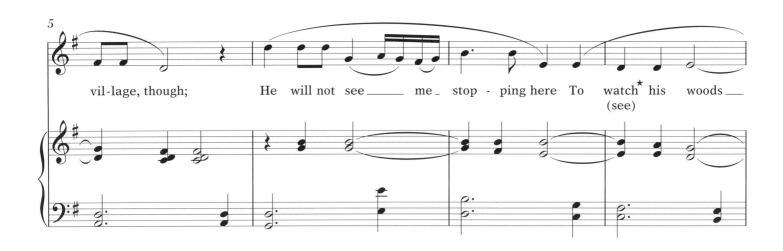

vil-lage, though; He will not see ____ me _ stop - ping here To watch* his woods ____ (see)

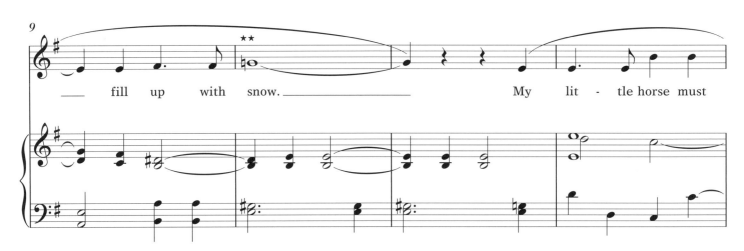

____ fill up with snow. _____ My lit - tle horse must

*"Watch" in Frost's poem, changed by Barber to "see."

**This dissonance is as marked in the manuscript; Barber may have intended to write a G-sharp in the vocal line.

Who carries corn and crown
original key

Robert Horan

Samuel Barber
c. 1942

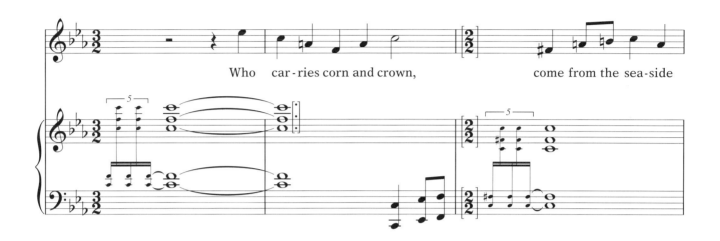

Who car-ries corn and crown, come from the sea-side

down, de - stroy-er of my town. And

in the halls of wheat hear you his ser - pent feet

Barber indicated no tempo or dynamics in his manuscript. Barber shows 32nd notes in the 5 figures in the first few bars. We believe this to be a simple error, and have corrected them to be 16th notes.

tomb. His head of love, his

hands of lace un- winds my fi - nal

___ hid - ing place. ___

Three Songs: The Words from Old England
1. Lady, when I behold the roses
original key: E Major

Anonymous

Samuel Barber
1925

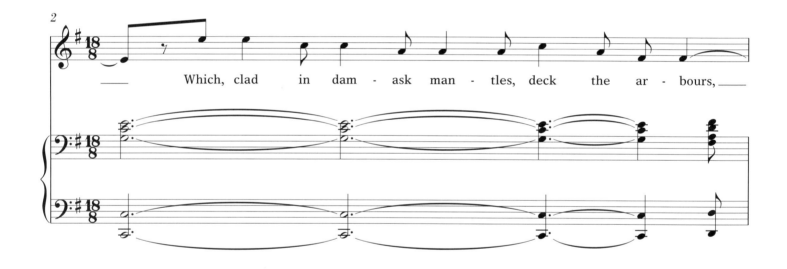

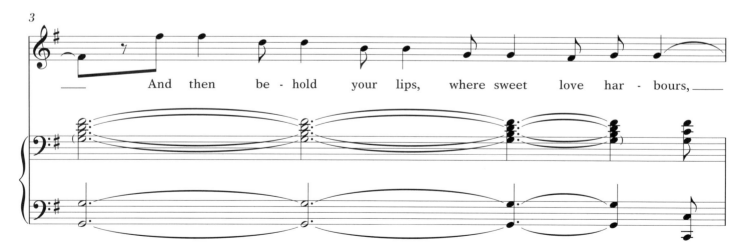

There are no dynamics in Barber's manuscript.

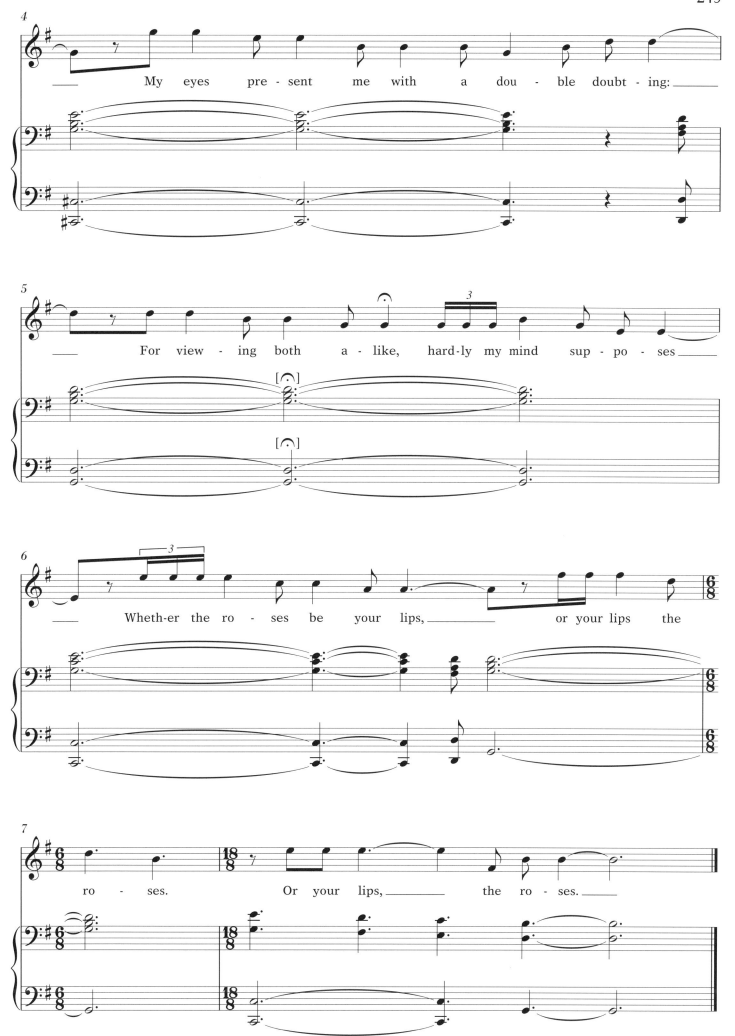

2. An Earnest Suit to His Unkind Mistress Not to Forsake Him

original key: E minor

Thomas Wyatt

Samuel Barber
1926

*"That" in Wyatt's poem, changed by Barber to "Who."

*See footnote on previous page.

thus And have no more pit - y____ Of him that lov - eth thee?____ A -
(On)*

las,____ thy cru - el - ty!____

And wilt thou leave me thus?____ Say

nay,____ say nay,____ say nay!

*"Of" in Wyatt's poem, changed by Barber to "On."

3. Hey nonny no!

original key: C Major

Anonymous (16th century)

Samuel Barber
1926

With boisterous good-humor!

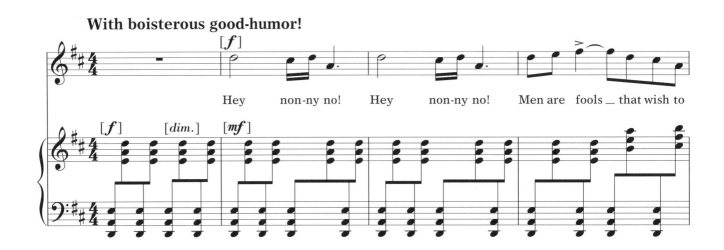

Hey non-ny no! Hey non-ny no! Men are fools __ that wish to

die! _____

Is't not fine to dance and sing ___

When the bells of death do ring?

There are no dynamics in Barber's manuscript; minimal suggestions have been made.

Is't not fine to swim in wine, ___ And turn up-on the toe, ___

And sing ___ hey non-ny no! When the winds blow and the seas flow?

Hey non-ny no! ___ Hey non-ny no! Hey non-ny no!

Men are fools ___ that wish to die! ___

To G. S. Aunt Bess

Thy Love
original key

Elizabeth Barrett Browning

Samuel Barber
1926

[**Moderato**]

If thou wouldst love me, let it be for naught

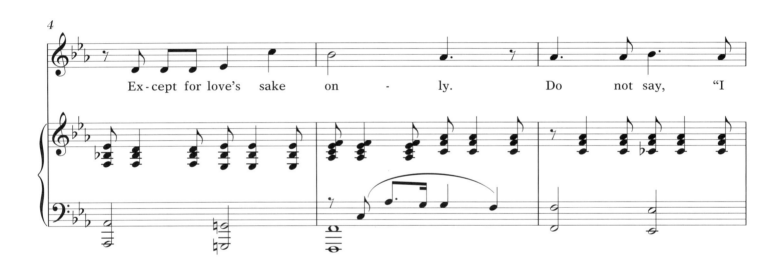

Ex-cept for love's sake on - ly. Do not say, "I

love her for her smile— her way of speak - ing gent - ly. For

Barber indicated no tempo or dynamics in his manuscript.

Two Poems of the Wind
1. Little Children of the Wind
original key

Fiona Macleod (William Sharp)

Samuel Barber
1924

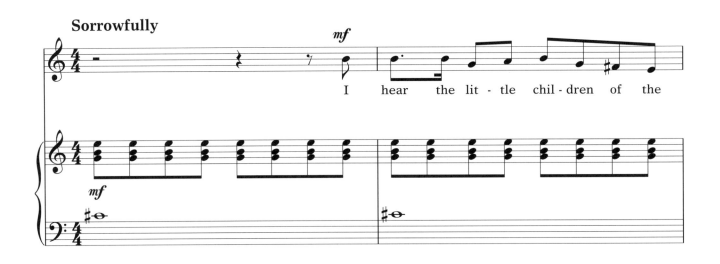

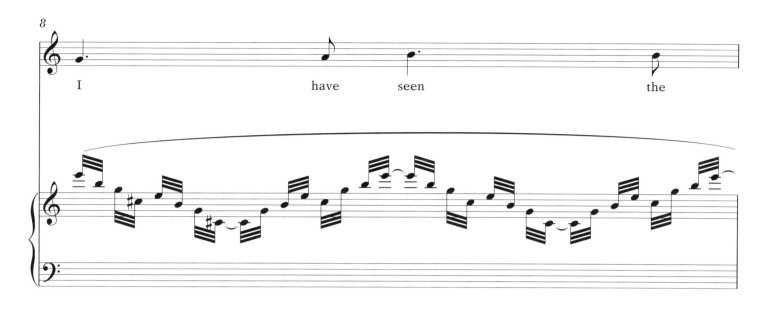

I have seen the

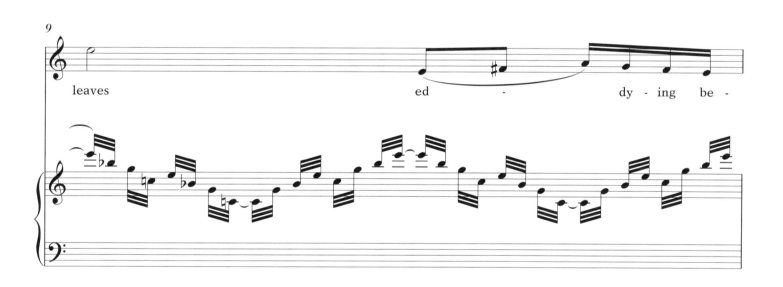

leaves ed - dy - ing be -

Lento

tenderly

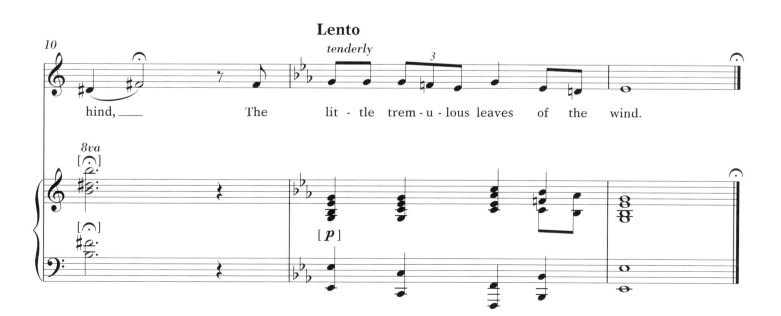

hind,___ The lit - tle trem - u - lous leaves of the wind.

2. Longing

original key

Fiona Macleod (William Sharp)

Samuel Barber
1924

Allegro con grazioso

O __ would I were __ the cool __ wind __ that's blow - ing from __ the

sea, _____ Each lone - liest val - ley I would search till I should come to __

Tempo I

me— The grey si-lence, the grey waves,— the grey waste of the sea.— O— would I were— the cool— wind— that's blow-ing from— the sea.— Each lone-liest val-ley I would search till I— should come to thee.

*The optional note appears in Barber's manuscript.

Two Songs of Youth
1. Invocation to Youth
original key: C Major

Laurence Binyon

Samuel Barber
1925

With fire*

ff

Come, then, as ev - er, like the Wind _____ at

(2)

morn - ing! Joy - ous, O Youth, in the a - ged (an)**

4

world re - new Fresh - ness to feel the e - ter - ni - ties a -

*"With fire" is Barber's only tempo indication; the busy figure in the second and twelfth measures makes a tempo of ♩ = 63 about as fast as is reasonable.
**"The" in Binyon's poem, changed by Barber to "an."

2. I never thought that youth would go

original key

Jessie B. Rittenhouse

Samuel Barber
1925

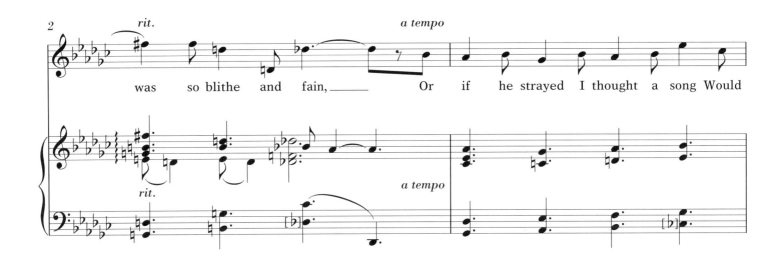

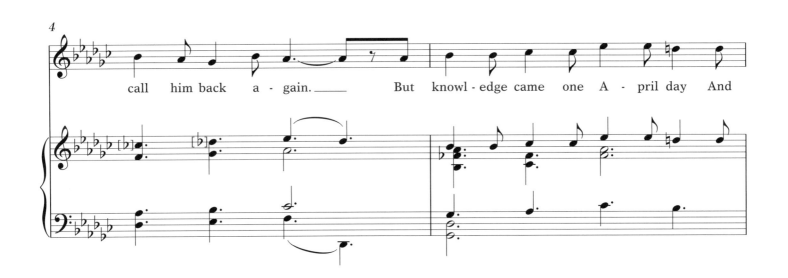

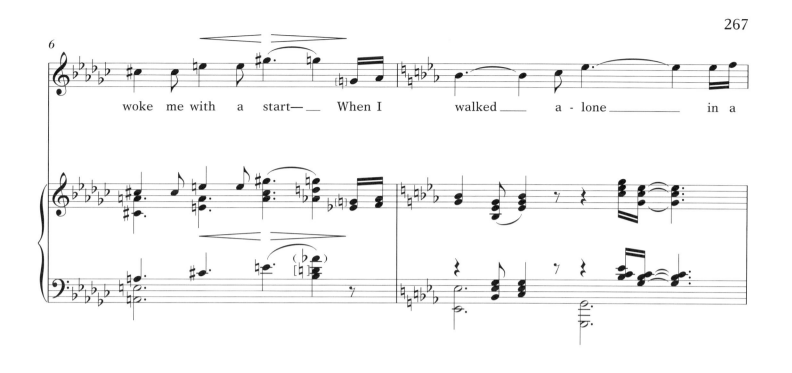

woke me with a start— When I walked a - lone in a

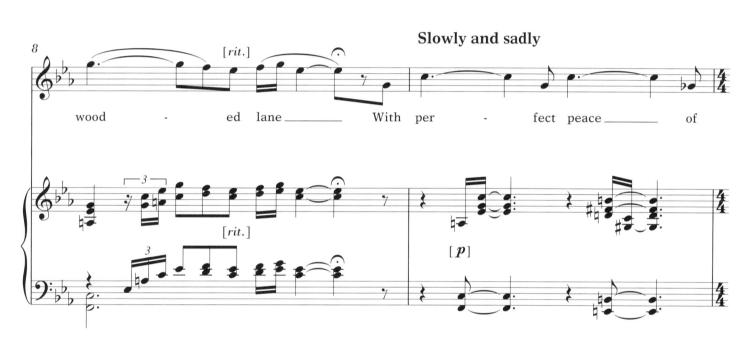

Slowly and sadly

wood - ed lane With per - fect peace of

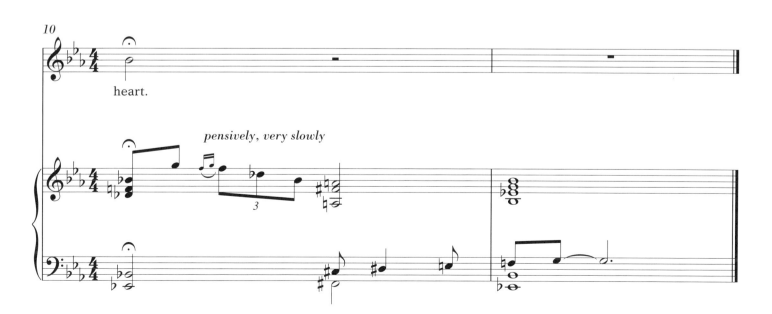

heart.

pensively, very slowly

Watchers
original key

Attributed to Dean Cornwell

Samuel Barber
1926

The manuscript of this free composition, without meter, is rather sketchy, and does not include rests to account for rhythm.
There is no tempo indicated, although a free recitative style is implied.

men to be sing - in' the songs of the seas and the ships! For

they don't have to light the white can - dles and bite back the

screams from their lips. _____

Tis them who be fight - in' the dev - ils that

*Barber wrote "etc." in this measure. We assume he means to repeat the material from the previous occurrence of the text.

APPENDIX 1:
MANUSCRIPT FACSIMILES OF
SELECTED EARLY SONGS

I Do Not Like Thee, Dr. Fell.

Low in B♭   High in D♭

Now in ninth edition
— 678,000 sold —

Dere Two Fella Joe

An encore Song in French-Canadian
Dialect —

The words related to the composer by a
White Mountain Guide —
Spoken by a French-Canadian father, very
much excited and mystified by
the arrival of twins
in his family

The music by

Sam Barber

Dedicated to Glenoke

Composed at Camp Wyanotie, Wolfeboro,
N.H. July, 1924.

Dere Two Fella Joe

More excitedly

cres - - - - - - - -, - , - .

Steck-a-yo' fing-a in Joe's mout', a-

ff

Confidentially

ha! She bite! Das Æste!

ff

Dere (there are) pronounced "Dare"
Joe ———— pronounced with a soft
st (equivalent to the French "J" as Zshoe
French "s'appelle") pronounced "such"
mout' ———— omit the "h"

October Weather

Samuel Barber. 25.

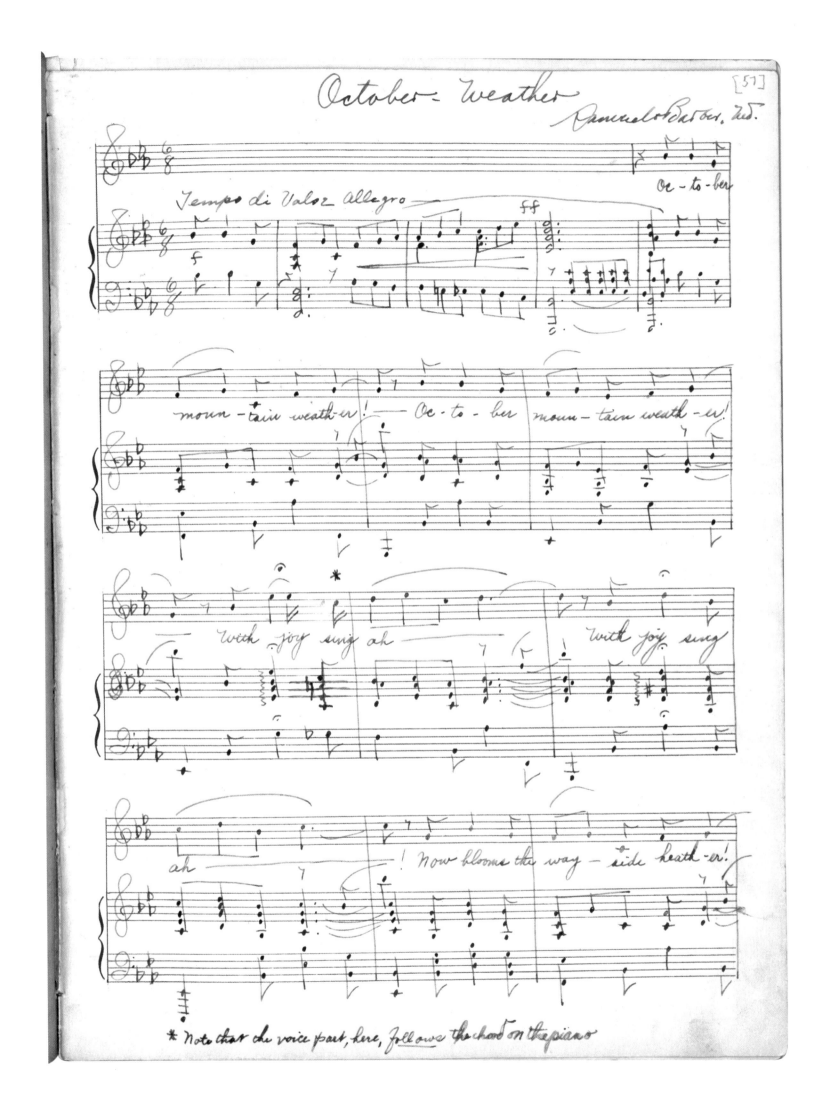

*Note that the voice part, here, follows the chord on the piano

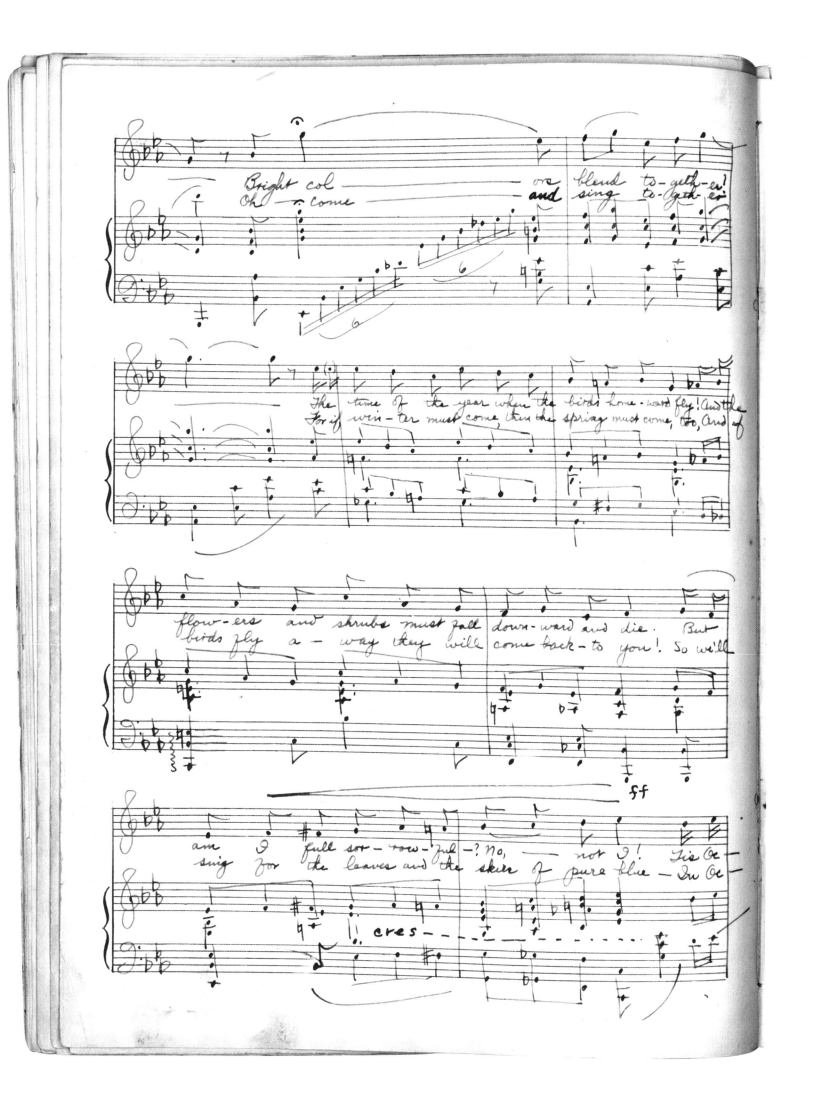

APPENDIX 2:
THE DAISIES
(ORIGINAL VERSION)

To Daisy

The Daisies
Original Version

James Stephens

Samuel Barber
1927

Allegretto con grazia

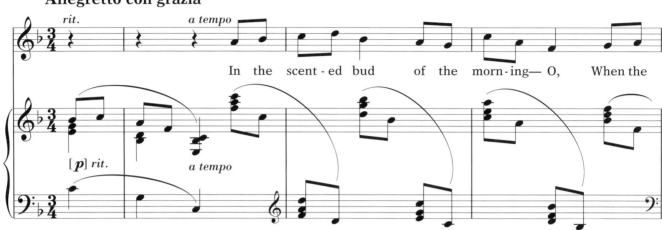

*In Stephens' poem the word is "happily," which Barber chose to set on two notes rather than three.